# The Music of Heaven

By

John Thurber
Cari Haus

Printed By

Remnant Publications

The Music of Heaven

This edition published 2001

Cover Photos by Photo Disc

Printed in the United States of America

ISBN  0-9711197-0-8

# A Special Word of Thanks

I couldn't have lived the life I've lived or done all the things I've done without Patsy, and this book wouldn't be complete without a tribute to her. She's been both a wonderful wife to me, and a "mother in Israel" to our children. Patsy spent many hours helping me with this book, and I'm also very grateful to her for that.

Thanks, Patsy, for being so good to me. By being right by my side, an active part in my ministry, you've made my years in God's work so much happier than they would have been otherwise. We are now in our forty-seventh year of marriage. Praise the Lord.

Thank you, Cari, for the countless hours you have put in to organize and smooth out this book. I could not have done it without your creative writing in just the right places. God has blessed you with a gift to honor Him.

Another thanks goes to Pastor Richard Wuttke, who sang in a quartet with me many years ago. Pastor Wuttke shared the tape of a wonderful talk on music he had given to some of his students. His thoughts had an impact on this book, and so I want to thank him for his contribution.

I'd also like to thank:

- Dwight Hall and Scott Erb of Remnant Publications for their time spent and helpful comments in shaping this book
- Judy Sherwin and Leila VanderMolen for taking the time to read *The Music of Heaven* and make suggestions early in the book's development, and
- Forrest Hilton, CPA, who, along with Patsy, spent many hours helping to proofread this book.

I'm sure there are others I could and should thank, but I owe a special word of praise to my Heavenly Father for giving me the strength and desire to put these thoughts into print. My heartfelt desire is that He will now bless it, leading many souls to appreciate the most heavenly music through the principles they find in these pages.

John Thurber

# Contents

*Sometimes I hear strange music,*
*Like none e're heard before,*
*Come floating softly earthward*
*As thro' heav'n's open door:*

*It seems like angel voices,*
*In strains of joy and love,*
*That swell the mighty chorus*
*Around the throne above.*

*O sweet, celestial music,*
*Heard from a land afar—*
*The song of Heav'n and Homeland,*
*Thru' doors God leaves ajar.*

—*A Song of Heaven and Homeland*
by Ira D. Sankey and E. E. Rexford

# Introduction

As I pen this book, there's no doubt in my mind that Jesus is coming very soon. Even the world seems to be in a state of expectancy, sensing that something spectacular is about to happen. The most incredible struggle of all time, this all-out war we've come to know as the "great controversy," is about to end.

As students of the Bible, you and I can have some insights into these things that others do not have. In the beautiful words of Paul, we are not in darkness, for we are "children of the light." (1 Thessalonians 5:5)

As children of the light, we are to have no fellowship with the works of darkness, for the "night is far spent" and "the day is at hand." We are therefore to "cast off the works of darkness, and...put on the armour of light." (Romans 13:12)

Then we will be His chosen generation, a royal priesthood, showing forth the praises of He who has called us "out of darkness into his marvelous light." (1 Peter 2:9)

As Christians, you and I are faced with the challenge of discerning between right and wrong, light and darkness, truth and error. And we have some real choices to make, for we live in a world full of Satan's influence, a world full of darkness that could very easily separate us from the love of Jesus Christ.

Unfortunately, this life-or-death struggle between the powers of good and evil has extended into the realm of the beautiful, the wonderful world of music. As I look back over the chapters of my own experience, the enormous power of music to change and influence hearts— either for good or evil—shines through again and again. In fact, one of the biggest challenges I faced as a youth evangelist, and still face today, is "what type of music should I pick?"

This is a difficult question, and not to be taken lightly. However, there is a series of solid, Bible-based principles that can help as we face these challenging choices. Having learned many of these principles through my years of involvement in music, I would like to share them in this book.

Studying the music of heaven has been a lifelong hobby of mine. The things I've learned on this important topic have really been quite life-changing to me, and may well be important for you as well. In this book, *The Music of Heaven*, I will be sharing what I've learned about the music in that grand and spectacular place.

I'd also like to give you some practical guidelines for choosing the best in music. We are not talking about rules and regulations here, but a group of easy-to-understand, heaven-sent principles you can understand and apply in your life.

Finally, I'd like to give you some "points to ponder" regarding some of the more controversial topics in music today. Don't worry, I have a soft touch. But these are perilous times we live in, and you need to be informed.

In the end, you're the one who will choose the music that weaves in, through, and around your life. Be assured that whatever you choose will have an impact on your character. If you ever doubt that fact, please read the stories at the end of this book. Many of them demonstrate the power of music, a power I've seen in action on countless occasions.

Many times, just before the King's Heralds sang, we prayed that if possible the very angels of heaven would join in our song. Later, people would come up to us and say, "I don't know what it was about your singing tonight. I've never heard anything like it before. The Lord must have really blessed you tonight."

In music, the physical phenomenon where a pure sound or note can awaken another musical note is known as an overtone. When the sound is very pure, one string can actually awaken another! The awakened overtone, which is often one octave higher, sympathizes, harmonizes and blends with the music without being actually played. It's interesting to "note" that only related strings, those that harmonize with each other, may result in these rich and resonant musical tones.

Perhaps this is what happened with Lucifer's pure voice, which resonated so sweetly that he actually sang in harmony with himself. Perhaps this is what happened with the King's Heralds and numerous other musical groups, when the hearers felt sure they had heard angels sing. For as our hearts sing out the praises of heaven, notes of grandeur are awakened not only around us, but in the courts of heaven above.

Of course, if we wish to awaken the music of heaven, we must have some idea of what it's like. If we wish to sing on the Sea of Glass, we must take time to tune up now. Who knows, if we listen carefully to that strange yet wonderful music, music "like none e'er heard before, come floating softly earthward as through heaven's open door," our thoughts and hearts may be carried to courts above. Then, having harmonized with heaven's music, we'll have no trouble knowing the song of our Shepherd, for we are very familiar with His voice.

This is the experience I long for in my own life, and wish for each reader of this book. Then together we can say, with Joshua and so many other noble characters that followed in his train, "Choose ye this day whom you will serve, but as for me and my house, we will serve the Lord."

See you on the Sea of Glass!

—John Thurber

*Now soft, and low and restful,*
*It floods my soul with peace,*
*As if God's benediction*
*Bade all earth's trouble cease.*

*Then grander than the voices,*
*Of wind, and wave, and sea—*
*It fills the dome of heaven*
*With glorious harmony.*

*O sweet, celestial music,*
*Heard from a land afar,*
*The song of Heav'n and Homeland,*
*Thru' doors God leaves ajar!*

*—A Song of Heaven and Homeland*
*by Ira D. Sankey and E. E. Rexford*

# 1

# The View From Down Here

*This book is about the music of heaven, and I won't disappoint you. If you want to look up, however, it helps to know where you are standing. We have to put things in perspective, which is why I've chosen to write one "earthly" chapter here at the start of this book. Then, with our feet solidly planted on this planet, we can look up together—to that beautiful place where we all hope to go, and the wonderful music of heaven.*

Once upon a time and quite a few years ago, before I was old enough to play or sing or even open my eyes, music surrounded my body. My tiny ears caught the rhythm of my dear mother's heart, picked up the vibrations as she hummed little tunes, learned the sound of her sweet, mellow voice.

Life was simple then. I was cozy and snug and warm, soothed by the rhythm of sounds all around me. So it was a comfort to me, when I first debuted in this world, to still hear the sound of my own mother's voice.

She was a singer, my mother. One of five singing sisters who sang all over New England, mostly at campmeetings and churches. My father was musical too, with a sweet tenor voice that some match-maker noticed would blend quite well with my mother's. They were asked to sing a duet, and the rest, as they say, is somewhat historic.

Mom and Dad blended their voices, then lives, and I, together with Wayne and Virginia, came out of that wonderful union. I was somewhat of a surprise, it seems, for Wayne was eight when I arrived on the scene. But there weren't many surprises about the way I was raised. My parents were loving but firm, and my life, as you might expect, was filled with wonderful music.

I can still remember that first song I sang, standing in front of a church at the ripe old age of three. It was an evangelistic series, and I had been asked to lead in a hymn. I swung my arm like a softball pitcher to lead the church in that song. It was a wonderful moment for me, and even at that young age, one I will never forget.

My childhood was filled with learning and fun, ballgames and school and the usual round of mischievous boyish pranks. My mother was loving but firm, and my dad—well, he had the softer touch. Their love was a constant in my life, for they prayed with me, played with me, and taught me to know my Savior. And through my childhood days the thread that ran so true, with a stitch just in time to save me from some childish mischief, was the wonderful gift of good music.

Sometimes we sang while we played, sometimes we sang while we worked. Friday nights were a specially tender time. There was no rush to bring in the Sabbath, for we were ready, seated in the parlor and waiting, one half hour before sundown. It was a silent time, those last few minutes as the clocked ticked away. A quiet time to reflect on the week just past. Then, as the sun sank into the west, I felt the Holy Spirit warming my very soul. In a very special way, God had come. He was there with my family, welcoming us into Sabbath rest.

When the sky was aflame with crimson and the sun could no more be seen, my mother would lead us to the piano. Then, oh how we sang. Praise to God and thanks to His name were the themes of our songs. I learned to sing parts round that piano, and I learned to sing like I meant it. Many times I saw the tears of my father spilling down his cheeks as the meaning of some special hymn touched the chords of his heart. The angels were singing with us too, for they love to join in when we sing with feeling.

The music of my childhood was enriched when I went to school. My mother despaired of teaching me piano, for my mitt was always under the bench during practice, waiting for chances to run out and play.

"You'll be sorry someday," she warned when I quit, and I am. But I never could quite quit singing, and my teachers didn't give me the opportunity, either. They loved to sing hymns, and though one in particular had far from a solo voice, you could see the love of Jesus written all over his face when he sang those sacred tunes and he taught me much about worship and song.

I sang in my first quartet while in sixth grade, and, much to my joy and amazement, was asked to sing first tenor in the Atlantic Union College Quartet when in the ninth grade. As it turned out, that was just one more step down the road towards a life that's been filled with music.

I could regale you with stories of the college quartets I sang in, singing with the King's Heralds and what it was like to work with H.M.S. Richards, Sr. I'd love to tell you the tales I've told at Weeks of Prayer and campmeetings all over this country—stories of the "shoeshine boy," the fat lady from the circus, and the crowd that didn't clap. But though I've tucked some favorite stories in at the end of this book, that's not my real purpose in writing this tome. I want to introduce you to a lifelong passion of mine, a topic I've studied for years, the song that's become so real to me every day of my life.

It is music that I hear, not the discord and clanging so often heard on this earth, but a sweet and special, soft and melodious music. Floating over the gates of a faraway city, it wafts down through light years of space and touches our hearts on this earth. If you've never heard it before, or haven't listened lately, you might have to cup your hands over your ears to pick up its sweet, soft tones. But it is there, playing softly, wooing hearts and inviting us all to explore its treasures. It's the music—the beautiful music of heaven.

# The Music of Heaven

*This music haunts me ever,*
*Like something heard in dreams—*
*It seems to catch the cadence*
*Of heav'nly winds and streams,*

*My heart is filled with rapture,*
*To think, some day to come,*
*I'll sing it with the angels*
*The song of heav'n and home.*

*O sweet, celestial music,*
*Heard from a land afar—*
*The song of Heav'n and Homeland,*
*Thru' doors God leaves ajar!*

—*A Song of Heaven and Homeland*
by Ira D. Sankey and E. E. Rexford

# 2

# The Beautiful Music of Heaven

If you've ever been downtown in New York or Chicago or some other very large city, you know the sights and sounds that throb through the streets of that place. There are taxis cutting in and out, horns honking, and people scurrying down miles and miles of sidewalks. There are engines revving, tires squealing, and policemen blowing their whistles at the endless rounds of hub-bub. Running through it all is the murmur of human voices, some talking, some shouting, and some blaring broadcasts out of a thousand rolled-down windows. These are the sounds of an earthly city—and it's hard for us to imagine anything else.

We must try to imagine, however, if we would glimpse the glories of that wonderful place called Heaven. We must take our eyes off the asphalt, and think gold. We must pull our shoulders from the jostling crowds, and consider courteous, friendly hands yielding the right-of-way. We must trade in our trusty cab driver for a brand new set of wings, say good-bye to the smog and travel backwards, backwards in time. And yes, we must close our ears to the bleeping, blasting and blaring that fills the air of all earthly cities.

For we are in Heaven now, and our hearts have left this place. It's warm in Heaven, for a soft glow of light encircles the beautiful city. There are no exhaust fumes, no piles of dirty snow, just greenery, gold streets, and shimmering precious stones. There are angels here, majestic beings with strong bodies, sure steps and wings. A soft halo of light encircles the gates of Heaven, reflecting the peace that permeates every nook of that place.

High above the city, under an emerald rainbow, is a gorgeous white throne, the throne of God Himself. You can't go into the throne room, but you watch as the angels go there. As they approach its door, you see them stepping softly, covering their faces, assuming an utmost attitude of reverence mingled with love. And you know that this God, this God whom the angels serve, must be incredibly special.

Having seen some of the sights in Heaven, you now sit down on a park bench to take in the sounds of the city. And what sounds they are! The angels passing in front of your bench all talk in musical voices. Some are deep and resonant, others silvery, but all have a certain richness that you just haven't heard on earth. You could think they were all great singers, and judging from the intricate tunes they hum as they work, indeed they are.

One singer in particular seems to stand out from the rest. He is tall and noble, head and shoulders above the others, and seems to be rather important. You see him hurrying to and from the throne room, answering angel questions, and learn that his name is Lucifer. Then, much to your joy and amazement, you find that a heavenly concert is very soon to take place.

You watch as the angels roll out their harps, pick up their trumpets, and take their places on platforms and towers nearby. A quiet murmuring fills the air, together with the soft humming and strumming of ten thousand expert musicians. Then all is silent, for Lucifer raises his hand. Standing high on a platform where all the angels can see him, he looks more noble than ever.

Your attention is captured when Lucifer starts to sing. His voice is so rich and resounding, and, to your great amazement, floats over the gates of the city, singing in harmony with itself! Only for a few notes, of course, to start the oratorio. But the music is exquisite, unlike anything you've heard before.

Then, with a sweep of his mighty arm, Lucifer brings in half of the heavenly choir. The sound is so spectacular, so full and glorious, it sends a shiver right up your spine. This is an antiphonal angel anthem, with a troupe of trumpeters posing their musical question from across the way, an ensemble of harp players answering from somewhere across the River of Life, and a massive choir of angels tying it all together with thousands of golden voices. And through it all the voice of Lucifer can be heard above the rest, adding an obbligato here, a trill there, and a special note someplace else.

The theme of the song is praise, of course—praise to the great God of the Universe for His goodness and grace and love. That's what the angels love to sing about, for they truly love God. In spite of their remarkable beauty, gorgeous voices, and many other gifts, the angels appear amazingly humble.

When this spectacular rendition of musical genius strikes its last chord and finally fades into silence, your human heart leaps for a standing ovation. Your hands are five inches apart, ready to thunder a round of applause, when your thoughts are interrupted by thousands of jubilant angel voices.

"Praise God!" "Hallelujah!" and "Glory to His name!" ring through the streets of Heaven. Scanning the angel choir, you see faces filled with the joy of a perfect performance—yet no one seems to want praise! Then your eyes travel up to Lucifer, composer, arranger, and conductor of the whole spectacular affair. He is bowing now—not towards any intended audience, but to the great God of the universe.

Your human heart wonders that Lucifer doesn't seem to take any credit for this extraordinary performance. In your minds eye you can see your own self on that platform, having just orchestrated one of the greatest musical events in heavenly history. To the self-ish human heart, it would seem only fitting to take a slight bow. To accept just one round of applause for a job that's very well done. Then your mind is brought gently back to the realities of Heaven as Lucifer's gorgeous voice rings out once more, rising majestically above the angel choir.

"Praise God!" he is saying. "Praise God!"

### Notable Quotes:

"…All the morning stars sang together and all the sons of God shouted for joy." (Job 38:7)

"Music forms a part of God's worship in the courts above, and we should endeavor, in our songs of praise, to approach as nearly as pos-sible to the harmony of the heavenly choirs. The proper training of the voice is an important feature in education and should not be neglected. Singing, as a part of religious service, is as much an act of worship as is prayer. The heart must feel the spirit of the song and give it right expression." (*Patriarchs and Prophets* page 594)

"I saw the beauty of heaven. I heard the angels sing their rapturous songs, ascribing praise, honor, and glory to Jesus. I could then realize something of the wondrous love of the Son of God." (*Testimonies* Volume 1 page 123)

*Shall we gather at the river,*
*Where bright angel feet have trod,*
*With its crystal tide forever*
*Flowing by the throne of God?*

*Yes, we'll gather at the river,*
*The beautiful, the beautiful river,*
*Gather with the saints at the river*
*That flows by the throne of God.*

—by Robert Lowry

# 3

# Discord in Paradise

We know from biblical history that at some point in his life, Lucifer really did crave applause. His heart was "lifted up because of his beauty," and, who knows, it could be that his extraordinary musical talents had something to do with the pride in his heart as well.

Whatever its source, God's mightiest angel watered a little seed of pride 'til it grew into a mighty tree of selfishness. His exclamations of "Praise God" and "Glory to His name" were gradually replaced by self-satisfied smiles. Perhaps he started by giving a slight nod to the angel audience after a particularly spectacular solo, then a slight bow, before finishing with a flourish of encores, bows and more encores.

Then Lucifer, leader of the angelical choir, musician extraordinaire and the noblest of all the angels, sounded a new note in heaven. It was a discordant note, a rebellious note, so unlike the harmonious loving thoughts that had filled his heart before.

The din of sin was foreign music to Heaven. No doubt it seemed to the faithful angels as if thousands of honking horns—all tooting loudly in a slightly different pitch—had invaded the streets of Heaven in one decadent, discordant caravan.

In His great mercy, God allowed the attempted angel coup to progress for quite some time. He loved Lucifer, and wanted to win him back. But it was not to be, for Lucifer refused to change his mind. Worse yet, he took one third of the angels with him.

That was a big blow to the music of heaven. The choir must have been saddened to see so many they loved deceived by pride and self-centeredness.

Lucifer had never intended to lose heaven. He thought he would win some concessions from God, or even take God's place on the throne! But in time he found himself, and his angels, outside of the pearly gates.

This must have affected his music. It seemed he had lost his song, or at the very least, the main topic of his songs. Until now, his songs had praised the goodness and grace of God. But now he was angry with God! His bitterness soon seeped into his music, as the seeds of rebellion simmered and brewed in his heart.

As heaven's former most-talented musician, he still knew the recipe for good music. But this made him all the more dangerous, for he could disguise wrong songs. No doubt this diabolical talent was particularly helpful in keeping the fallen angels united. Any semblance of goodness left in their souls could soon be erased by the driving beat of a rousing rebel tune. The one who had once written heavenly music to unite the angelical choir in love and adoration to their Maker, now bent his best talents to honor his own wayward soul. Together with his angel army, he marched toward the beat of an even greater rebellion.

It was into this atmosphere, a universe torn by the entrance of sin, that God brought his two newest children. They were protected from Lucifer. He did not have the run of their beautiful Eden home. But Lucifer's rebellion did alter the landscape of Eden. For like every other world in the universe, citizens of this beautiful garden would now have to make a choice. It was a simple choice, or at least, God tried to make it that way. But it was a choice, no less, at a tree in the midst of the garden.

This tree, the Tree of Knowledge of Good and Evil, was the only place Lucifer could go. And it was while there, in this tree, that Lucifer was reminded so vividly of what he had lost in heaven. From his perch on a limb he could see happy angelic faces, faces he had once known. He saw the smiles of Adam and Eve, and their love for each other, God, and the angels. But most infuriating of all, he heard their music. Perhaps they sang songs that he had once written himself. Perhaps it was his favorite hymn or anthem, a beautiful chorus that had once inspired him to greater adoration of God, that now drove him to deeper hatred.

The songs had not changed. It was Lucifer who had changed.

In his search to become higher, he had sunk to the depths of sin and despair. There was no hope for him now. He had closed the door to God's mercy: Lucifer had become Satan. And so, enraged at the beautiful music that he himself had once loved, Satan vowed to halt the happiness on this earth. His discordant words and actions had already altered the music of heaven. Now he wanted to stop it for good.

### *Notable Quotes:*

"In the beginning, God was revealed in all the works of creation. It was Christ that spread the heavens, and laid the foundations of the earth. It was His hand that hung the worlds in space, and fashioned the flowers of the field. It was He that filled the earth with beauty, and the air with song. And upon all things in earth, and air, and sky, He wrote the message of the Father's love." (*Desires of Ages* page 20)

"The angels...united with Adam and Eve in holy strains of harmonious music, and as their songs peeled forth from blissful Eden, Satan heard the sound of their strains of joyful adoration to the Father and Son. And as Satan heard it his envy and hatred and malignity increased and he expressed his anxiety to his followers to incite them to disobedience and at once bring down the wrath of God upon them and change their songs of praise to hatred and curses to their Maker." (*Story of Redemption* page 31)

"The heart in harmony with God is lifted above the annoyances and trials of this life. But a heart where the peace of Christ is not, is unhappy, full of discontent; the person sees defects in everything, and he would bring discord into the most heavenly music." (*Testimonies* Volume 5 page 488)

*Were you there when they crucified my Lord?*
*Were you there when they crucified my Lord?*

*O———!*
*Sometimes it causes me to tremble,*
*tremble,*
*tremble.*

*Were you there when they crucified my Lord?*

—American Negro Spiritual

# 4

# The Day Heaven's Music Stopped

As history records, Satan did stop the music of heaven. By engineering the fall of Adam and Eve, he brought such sadness to the celestial courts that no one, not one single angel felt like even humming a tune. If there were birds in heaven, they must have stopped singing too. Except for a few hushed whispers, the sounds of angel feet walking, or doors opening and closing, heaven was very silent indeed.

That's when a very beautiful thing happened, an act so heroic that angels gasped in amazement. For then, in that dim, dark hour, Jesus offered to save the world.

It took the angels a while to grasp the idea. They loved Jesus with all their hearts, and were loathe to give Him up. They knew He would go at great risk, and offered to die themselves. But Jesus explained to them that only He could save man. The cost of sin was so great, and God's law was so very holy, that only Jesus Himself could die in the sinner's place.

When all the hubbub had died down in heaven, some of the angels started to feel like singing again. And they had a new song to sing, for they loved God now more than ever before. Though they'd always known He was loving and kind and good, they hadn't known He would stoop this low to save His fallen creation.

A new and noble angel had been chosen in Lucifer's place. Blessed with abundant musical talent, he assembled the heavenly harpists, singers and trumpeters for their first performance after the fall of man. Perhaps he, or another angel, had written a special number just for this happy occasion. As sinless angels, they could never know the depths of joy that humans would feel when pulled from the pit of sin. But they could share in that joy. They could sing of that joy. And so now, in tribute to the wonderful and now saving power of God, harps and trumpets and silvery voices flooded all heaven once more.

This infuriated Satan. He had wanted to stop heaven's music for good; all he got was an intermission. No doubt he stormed back to his workshop to draw up his next set of plans.

He didn't know how long this conflict could go on, but one thing he knew; he intended to fight God as long as he could. He had earth as his playground now, and man as his sinful subjects. And he aimed to control the whole race, attacking any vestige of godliness that might be left in their lives.

He had already attacked on appetite, now he meant to enslave on that point. And he would teach men to worship trees, rocks, idols, himself—anything except God. He would inspire treachery and theft and murder. He would defile the sanctity of marriage and stomp on God's holy Sabbath. He would mix the common with the sacred, teaching men to hate and steal and lie. And yes, he—one of the greatest musicians the universe has ever known—would extend his nonstop, all-out, self-declared war against God into the realm of music.

This would be easy for him, for he knew so much about it. He had the basic "recipe" for heavenly music by memory, plus a thousand variations. Now he would add a whole new mix to the scheme. There would be variations of variations, and a whole brood of mixed-up mutants.

Perhaps the evil angels wondered what Satan was doing when he set out a thousand "pots" of good music. They didn't have to wait long to find out, however. One can just imagine him stationing two demons at each pot, then handing out packets of diabolical ingredients.

After heating each pot up to the desired temperature, or should we say, tempo, the demons dumped in their packets. Some pots got a bucket of badness, others just got tainted teaspoons. Satan didn't mind what each of them got, as long as there was some bad in each brew.

So he mixed good words with bad music, bad words with good music, and bad words with bad music in a thousand variations. When the pots were cooked to a diabolical perfection, Satan stored them deep in his evil arsenal. He would tinker with them more later, to be sure. But they would be one of his most potent and lethal weapons in the weeks, years and centuries to come.

### Notable Quotes:

"The fall of man filled all heaven with sorrow. The world that God had made was blighted with the curse of sin and inhabited by beings doomed to misery and death. There appeared no escape for those who had transgressed the law. Angels ceased their songs of praise throughout the heavenly courts." (*Patriarchs and Prophets* page 63)

"A love for music leads the unwary to unite with world lovers in pleasure gatherings where God has forbidden His children to go. Thus that which is a great blessing when rightly used, becomes one of the most successful agencies by which Satan allures the mind from duty and from the contemplation of eternal things." (*Patriarchs and Prophets* page 594)

*What wondrous love is this,*
*O my soul, O my soul?*
*What wondrous love is this,*
*O my soul?*

*What wondrous love is this?*
*That caused the Lord of bliss,*
*To bear the dreadful curse*
*For my soul, for my soul?*
*To bear the dreadful curse*
*For my soul.*

—Attr. To Alexander Means

# 5

# The War for This World Heats Up

If you've never heard of antiphonal music, that's when two or more groups of singers or instrumentalists answer each other from different sides of a church. It's difficult to pull off sometimes, but the result can be truly spectacular.

Unfortunately, there has been a discordant form of antiphonal music echoing down through the centuries. Imagine yourself as the audience, sitting on Planet Earth. From up above, through the gates of Heaven, floats the purest, most beautiful music your mind could ever imagine. It has variety, to be sure, but the end result is always to pull you upward. It helps you want to love God more, praise Him more, and even to set your life in order.

Just below you, however, lodged in a frightful chasm, is music from the abyss. Some songs are quite horrendous; others seem more confusing than anything else. In fact, except for a misleading phrase, overly hyped rhythm, or slightly off-base theology woven in here or there, you could almost call it good music.

And there you are in the middle, looking back and forth. You live close to the earthly music, hear it all the time, and even think you like some of it. But there's something about that heavenly music, too. It seems to be calling you home.

This choice between heavenly and earthly music is nothing new, of course. In fact, it's been going on since biblical times.

Some of today's pop stars like to think they've come up with a "new" sound, a sound that's never been heard before. But the wisest man who ever lived said "there is nothing new under the sun." And, given the extreme talent and intelligence of people before the flood and others throughout the ages, it seems likely that many "flavors" of music have made their way down through the centuries.

There is certainly "evil" music mentioned in the Bible. We don't know what rebel Israelites were humming when they built the golden calf, but it wasn't the Doxology. Moab's ladies hadn't heard of Mozart when they led the foolish Israelite men into seduction, then destruction, but they wouldn't have liked him anyway. Their sultry little solos most likely included some ancient version of "I Know I'll Never Love This Way Again," or something like that.

No doubt the airwaves during Elijah's time were filled with radio stations B.A.A.L. and A.H.A.B. With Jezebel as chief disc jockey, a round of new sound was bound to evolve on the Top 40 Songs of Transgression. Some say it was for political reasons, but "The Old Rugged Cross" never did make the charts.

Those weren't hymn-singers collected by Solomon during his great apostasy, and that wasn't "Before Jehovah's Awful Throne" you heard on the Plain of Dura—at least, not at first. It took more than a gorgeous dancer to win John the Baptist's head. Have you ever heard of a dance without music? Who knows what the title of Salome's top song would be, but one thing is for sure: she didn't dance to the tune of uplifting music.

On the "good" side of things, we hear Miriam and her brother leading the "Song of Moses" after God swept away the Egyptians. The Israelites used song to memorize Scripture, and God inspired King David and other writers to compose an entire hymn, or should we say, Psalms, book. Then there were the songs of Deborah; Mary, the mother of Jesus; the angels welcoming Baby Jesus' birth; and our Lord Himself with the disciples on the Thursday before the cross. No doubt strains of celestial music echoed over Jerusalem after our Lord's resurrection, for all the great events around the life of Christ were surrounded with music. Since that time martyrs have sung at the stake, Christians have encouraged themselves by singing spiritual songs, and children have been educated and edified—all through the wonderful gift of music.

"As the children of Israel, journeying through the wilderness, cheered their way by the music of sacred song, so God bids His children today gladden their pilgrim life. There are few means more effective for fixing His words in memory than repeating them in a song. And such song has wonderful power. It has power to subdue rude and uncultivated natures, power to quicken thought and to awaken sympathy, to promote harmony of action, and to banish the gloom and foreboding that destroy courage and weaken effort." (*Education* page 167, 168)

At the same time, "Satan is continually seeking to overcome the people of God by breaking down the barriers which separate them from the world..." (*Great Controversy* page 508)

"...Music is the idol which many professed Sabbathkeeping Christians worship. Satan has no objection to music if he can make it a channel through which to gain access to the minds of the youth..." (*Testimonies* Volume 1 page 506)

There is a special power in music. Sometimes it results from the lyrics, sometimes it comes from the music itself, or sometimes from a combination of the two. When Dr. Patricia Schuller interviewed more than 400 unwed teenage mothers, she found that the music that they listened to helped turn them on to pre-marital sex. So you see Satan has twisted an instrument of praise and glory to suit his own purposes, fostering disobedience and diverting praise that should be given to God alone to anyone or anything else.

On the opposite end of the spectrum, many prisoners of war have kept their sanity by singing hymns and gospel songs during their time of need. Music is also a powerful tool for the family at worship, as parents and children find specialness and spiritual bonding as they lift their voices to heaven. How precious it is to listen to the sweet voices of children expressing their love for Jesus.

Yes, there is a war going on, a hand-to-hand combat for the life of souls. This life-or-death struggle is being fought on many battlefields, including music. Satan knows that music can change your mood, and the mood of whole groups of people, so he uses this tool to his best advantage. At the same time, God uses heavenly music to draw His children home.

"But how can I know what's good music?" you may be asking. "There are so many flavors and types I hardly know what to think."

While it's true that Satan has done a masterful job of confusing the issue of music, the Lord has not left us desolate. Just as parents can pick the voice of their children out of a crowd, those who listen will hear the sweet voice of God.

God has gifted His people with some basic, biblical and very simple principles that can be applied not only to music, but to other aspects of our lives. To uncover some of these principles, and help you choose God-given music, is the task of the rest of this book.

## *Notable Quotes:*

"...Balaam knew that the prosperity of Israel depended upon their observance of the law of God, and that there was no way to bring a curse upon them but by seducing them to transgression. He now decided to secure to himself Balak's reward, and the promotion he desired by advising the Moabites what course to pursue to bring the curse upon Israel. He counseled Balak to proclaim an idolatrous feast in honor of their idol gods, and he would persuade the Israelites to attend, that they might be delighted with the music, and then the most beautiful Midianitish women should entice the Israelites to transgress the law of God, and corrupt themselves, and also influence them to offer sacrifice to idols. This Satanic counsel succeeded too well..." (*Spirit of Prophecy* Volume 6 page 326-327)

"...Beguiled with music and dancing, and allured by the beauty of heathen vestals, they cast off their fealty to Jehovah. As they united in mirth and feasting, indulgence in wine beclouded their senses and broke down the barriers of self-control. Passion had full sway; and having defiled their consciences by lewdness, they were persuaded to bow down to idols. They offered sacrifice upon heathen altars and participated in the most degrading rites." (*Patriarchs and Prophets* page 454)

"How often in our own day, is the love of pleasure disguised by a 'form of godliness'! A religion that permits men, while observing the rites of worship, to devote themselves to selfish or sensual grati-fication, is as pleasing to the multitudes now as in the days of Israel. And there are still pliant Aarons, who, while holding positions of authority in the church, will yield to the desires of the unconsecrated, and thus encourage them in sin." (*Patriarchs and Prophets* page 317)

"I collected for myself silver and gold and the treasure of Kings and provinces. I provided for myself male and female singers, and the pleasures of men, many concubines, then I became great and increased more than all who preceeded me in Jerusalem. My wisdom also stood by me and all that my heart did desire I did not refuse them and I did not withhold my heart from any pleasure for my heart was pleased." (Ecclesiastes 2:8-10)

"The same spirit was manifested at the sacrilegious feast of Belshazzar. There was glee and dancing, hilarity and singing carried to an infatuation that beguiled the senses. Then the indulgence in inordinate, lustful affections, all this mingled in that disgraceful scene. God had been dishonored; His people had become a shame in the sight of the heathen. Judgments were about to fall on the infatuated, besotted multitude. Yet God in His mercy gave them opportunity to forsake their sins." (Manuscript 19 page 111)

"When Christ was a child like these children here, He was tempted to sin, but He did not yield to temptation. As He grew older He was tempted, but the songs His mother had taught Him to sing came into His mind, and He would lift His voice in praise. And before His companions were aware of it, they would be singing with Him. God wants us to use every facility which Heaven has provided for resisting the enemy." (Manuscript 65, 1901)

After Jesus overcame the temptations of Satan in the wilderness, all heaven broke into song. "It was enough. Satan could go no further. Angels ministered to the Saviour. Angels brought Him food. The severity of this conflict no human mind can compass. The welfare of the whole human family and of Christ Himself was at stake. One admission from Christ, one word of concession, and the world would be claimed by Satan as his, and he the prince of the power of darkness, would, he supposed, commence his rule. There appeared unto Christ an angel from heaven, for the conflict ended. Human power was ready to fail. But all heaven sang the song of eternal victory." (*Selected Messages* Volume 1 page 95)

"And at the death of Jesus the soldiers had beheld the earth wrapped in darkness at midday; but at the resurrection they saw the brightness of the angels illuminate the night, and heard the inhabitants of heaven singing with great joy and triumph: Thou hast vanquished Satan and the powers of darkness; Thou hast swallowed up death in victory." (*Desire of Ages* page 780)

"As Jesus came forth from the sepulcher, those shining angels prostrated themselves to the earth in worship, and hailed Him with songs of victory and triumph." (*Early Writings* page 182)

"Only for a few moments could the disciples hear the angels' song as their Lord ascended, His hands outstretched in blessing. They heard not the greeting He received. All heaven united in His reception. His entrance was not begged. All heaven was honored by His presence." (*SDA Bible Commentary* Volume 6 page 1053)

"After we had passed safely through the water, my eyes were attracted to something strange in the air. I saw angels marching through the air singing with solemn, clear voices, For the great day of His wrath is come, and who shall be able to stand? Their voices rang through the air. Upon their shoulders they had mantles that reached to their feet..." (Manuscript Volume 16 page 171)

# The Music of Heaven

*Angels we have heard on high,*
*Singing sweetly o'er the plain,*
*And the mountains in reply,*
*Echoing their glorious strain.*

—Traditional

\* \* \*

*Christ the Lord is risen today,*
*Alleluia!*
*Sons of men and angels say,*
*Alleluia!*
*Raise your joys and triumphs high!*
*Alleluia!*
*Sing, ye heavens, and earth reply,*
*Alleluia!*

—Charles Wesley

# 6

# When the Message of Music is "Me"

**Principle#1: "Not I, but Christ, be honored loved exalted…"**

As we discussed in an earlier chapter, pride was the main reason for Satan's downfall. The Bible tells us that his heart was "lifted up" because of his beauty. (Ezekiel 28:17) Unfortunately, this problem of pride is still plaguing humans today.

Exalting Christ sounds natural enough, for it is the purported purpose of every religious song. Unfortunately, however, there are a lot of religious songs where the words "me", "myself" and "I" eclipse all other themes. Such songs are more concerned with satisfying self or making "me" feel better than exalting Christ and Him crucified.

This is anti-biblical, for Jesus Himself said "If any man will come after me, let him deny himself, and take up his cross, and follow me." (Matthew 16:24) Christ denied Himself so that we might be exalted. Christ Himself was not proud, He was never a "star," His life was anything but a "road show." He was never onstage, seeking applause. Rather, "being found in fashion as a man, he humbled himself, and became obedient unto death, even the death of the cross. Wherefore God also hath highly exalted him, and given him a name which is above every name: That at the name of Jesus every knee should bow, of things in heaven, and things in earth, and things under the earth." (Philippians 2:8-10)

"In the heart of Christ, where reigned perfect harmony with God, there was perfect peace. He was never elated by applause, nor dejected by censure or disappointment. Amid the greatest opposition and the most cruel treatment, He was still of good courage." (*Desire of*

*Ages* page 330) This is important to God's people as the great controversy rages on.

Unfortunately, the principle of non-exaltation rules out much of even the Christian music in our world today. Though the whole concept of "stardom" is opposed to Christian humility, even Christian musicians use Hollywood's methods of image-building and stardom-seeking in order to sell more CDs. In response, "fans" worship the ground the "stars" walk on. In the words of one Michael W. Smith fan who sang in a choir at one of his concerts:

"I didn't get to shake his hand, but I stood about six feet from him, and I wanted to reach out and touch him. It was the biggest thrill of my life as I stood there with my eyes fixed on him."

Why did this lady practically worship Smith? Perhaps she was taking the advice of one of his popular songs, "Love me Good." This song, which repeats the phrase "love me good" at least twenty-five times, also includes forms of the words "I" and "me" at least twenty-five more times.

Did you notice who is missing? The word God, or Jesus, is not in this purportedly Christian song at all! Smith never mentions God, or Jesus, as the answer, only asks his fans to "love me good" (which, according to the number of CDs he sells, they do!).

Michael W. Smith is not alone in the emphasis of "me," "myself," and "I." Indeed, much of today's Contemporary Christian Music (CCM) puts the performer on a pedestal, exalted by the fans and his or herself. When the spotlights come on and the electronic extravaganzas begin, it is not Christ who is featured onstage. Rather, it is a god who is more concerned about climbing in the charts than repentance or freedom from sin. The appeal of such stars is to create fans for themselves, rather than followers of a selfless Christ. They are more concerned with emotional highs than the still small voice, more concerned about money than the true manna.

Another good example of this is in the song "I Get on My Knees," played repeatedly on some Christian MTV-like channels. The video features many close-up shots of an attractive female singer, sometimes in a low-cut dress or on the beach. Although the song is supposed to be about prayer, it's plain to see that it's really about the singer. No doubt most viewers are more wrapped up in how pretty she is, or how well she can sing, or what outfit she will wear in the next shot than they are in thinking about the meaning and blessings of prayer.

The spirit of self-exaltation should be a big red flag when a Christian is choosing music. If the song is about me, myself and I, or if the recording artist is into hype, self-promotion and stardom, let the listener beware.

Pride is one of the seven sins God hates. We were not created for personal stardom, but to glorify Him. When our human hearts are tempted to seek star status, we should remember the terrible fall of Lucifer, the very first "star." We would also do well to consider the words of an old but timeless hymn:

> *Not I, but Christ be honored, loved, exalted;*
> *Not I, but Christ, be seen, be known, be heard;*
> *Not I, but Christ, in every look and action,*
> *Not I, but Christ, in every thought and word.*

—Fannie E. Bolton

### Notable Quotes:

"Praise no man; flatter no man; and permit no man to praise or flatter you. Satan will do enough of this work. Lose sight of the instrument, and think of Jesus. Praise the Lord. Give glory to God. Make melody to God in your hearts. Talk of the truth. Talk of the Christian's hope, the Christian's heaven." (*Evangelism* page 630)

"It is unsafe, by our words and actions, to exalt a brother or sister, however apparently humble may be his or her deportment. If they really possess the meek and lowly spirit which God so highly esteems, help them to retain it. This will not be done by censuring them nor by neglecting to properly appreciate their true worth. But there are few who can bear praise without being injured." (*Testimonies* Volume 3 page 185)

"...It is not man that is to be the object of attraction. It is not man that is to lift up himself. It is not man that is to glory or receive praise or glory, but the Lord God of Israel. All that man has—life, the means of existence, happiness, and other blessings unnumbered that come to him day by day—is from the Father above. Man is a debtor for all he proudly claims as his own. God gives His precious gifts, that they may be used in His service. Every particle of the glory of man's success belongs to God. It is His manifold wisdom that is displayed in the works of men, and to Him belongs the praise." (Ellen G. White 1888 Materials page 934)

"Gorgeous apparel, fine singing, and instrumental music in the church do not call forth the song of the angel choir. In the sight of God these things are like the branches of the unfruitful fig tree which bore nothing but pretentious leaves." (Manuscript page 123, 1899)

"Christ looks for fruit, for principles of goodness and sympathy and love. These are the principles of heaven, and when they are revealed in the lives of human beings, we may know that Christ is formed within, the hope of glory." (Manuscript page 123, 1899)

### *Point to Ponder:*

Who does my music center around? Me? The performer? Something else in this world—or God?

*We have not known Thee as we ought,*
*Nor learned Thy wisdom, grace, and power;*
*The things of earth have filled our thought,*
*And trifles of the passing hour.*

*Lord, give us light*
*Thy truth to see,*
*And make us wise*
*In knowing Thee.*

—Thomas B. Pollock

# 7

# Satan's Creative Counterfeits

**Principle #2:  Satan has a counterfeit for every one of God's gifts, and that includes even Christian music.**

God's original plan for music was to give His creatures a special outlet for praise, whether it was just one person or a whole heavenly host.  Music is the brush in the hands of the Master Artist, through which He can paint beautiful pictures on the canvas of our souls.  God gave us music because His creatures are the happiest when they praise Him, and music has always been God's chosen method of praise.

Satan's aim for music today is the same as it was when he heard Adam and Eve singing those beautiful songs.  He wants to bring praise and attention to anyone—or anything—but God.

The Devil is too smart to try and pervert Christian music openly.  His greatest plan is to appear as an "angel of light," which often makes it very difficult to see his music for what it really is.  Satan wants his music to be just as close to God's music as it can possibly be: he wants his counterfeit to look like the genuine! This is why Jesus called Satan the "Father of Lies," for deception has always been one of the Devil's best weapons in his all-out war for the world.

God has created many wonderful things for His children's joy and happiness.  These stir up Satan's envy, and so he produces a counterfeit.  Here are some examples:

- There is a true Sabbath—and a false.
- There is a true series of Christ centered doctrines—and there are false.

- There are genuine principles of family living—and false ones.
- There are genuine principles of pure biblical sexuality—and counterfeit ones.
- There is true worship—and false worship.
- There are biblical reasons for divorce—and there are false ones.
- There is music that truly is praise—and music that promotes false praise

By setting up a counterfeit system of Christian music, Satan has taken one of God's most useful devices for saving souls and crafted a delusion which, except for certain elements that somehow subtly pull us away from God, seems very much like the real thing. This is called mixing truth with error, and it's one of the hardest things for Christian to distinguish at times.

You'd think good mixed with error would be easy to see, but the Devil is too smart to try that. He is going to make sure the main ingredient in his music is some form of truth or beauty. Otherwise, the error would be easy to see and not one soul would be fooled. This challenge of truth mixed with error is a very real problem for our church today. It scares me to think of some of the choices we have to make, for the Devil is very crafty. But while the choices are scary, the solutions are also very comforting.

Christian music runs the full gamut today. Every kind of music imaginable comes in a religious, though not necessarily sacred, package. The Bible warns us about these deceptions in 1 John 4:1, (NKJ) "…Do not believe every spirit, but test the spirits to see whether they are of God; for many false prophets have gone out into the world." The Devil is in a race with Jesus for the hand of the church in marriage. As a result, every Christian must be on his or her guard.

In learning to detect counterfeit Christian music, we would do well to take a lesson from the FBI. Their system of training agents to spot counterfeit money seems to work pretty well. At the start of the training, they don't let the agents see any counterfeit money. Rather, they put them in a room with nothing but genuine money for a full three months. It may sound boring, but they study every detail of that genuine money until they know it by heart.

The big test comes at the end of three months, when the FBI brings in a whole bucket of money. Some of the money is fake, but it doesn't fool the new agents. They have seen so much of the genuine that the counterfeit shows up right away.

This is an important lesson for Christians. If we stay close enough to God, the counterfeits show up pretty quickly.

"But how can you know what is real and what is fake unless you have sampled everything?" some people want to know. Unfortunately, this is the same line Satan used with such success on Eve, in the Garden of Eden.

"Here is your problem, Eve," I can just hear him saying. "You haven't sampled everything yet!"

Detecting some counterfeits will always be a challenge for Christians, for Satan is a master at starring as an angel of light. He plans to destroy everyone that he can, for he really is a murderer and the Father of Lies. His goal is to divert us from praising God, and many of his captivating tricks are not so obvious. This is all the more reason to be on our guard at all times, and remember that we have this promise:

"There hath no temptation taken you but such as is common to man: but God is faithful, who will not suffer you to be tempted above that ye are able; but will with the temptation also make a way to escape, that ye may be able to bear it."(1 Corinthians 10:13)

### *Notable Quotes:*

"Satan...is in attendance when men assemble for the worship of God. Though hidden from sight, he is working with all diligence to control the minds of the worshipers. Like a skillful general, he lays his plans beforehand. As he sees the messenger of God searching the Scriptures, he takes note of the subject to be presented to the people. Then he employs all his cunning and shrewdness to control circumstances that the message may not reach those whom he is deceiving on that very point...some will be prevented from hearing the words that might prove to him a savor of life unto life." (*Great Controversy* page 518, 519)

"Good and evil never harmonize. Between light and darkness there can be no compromise. Truth is light revealed; error is darkness, righteousness has no fellowship with unrighteousness. The safety of the Christian is assured only when they work and sleep with their armor on." (Manuscript 82, 1900)

"Evil angels in the form of believers will work in our ranks to bring in a strong spirit of unbelief. Let not even this discourage you, but bring a true heart to the help of the Lord against the powers of Satanic agencies. These powers of evil will assemble in our meetings, not to receive a blessing, but to counterwork the influences of the Spirit of God." (*Last Day Events* page 161)

"There is an emotional excitement, a mingling of the true with the false, that is well adapted to mislead....Wherever men neglect the testimony of the Bible, turning away from those plain, soul-testing truths which require self-denial and renunciation of the world, there we may be sure that God's blessing is not bestowed." (*Great Controversy* page 464)

"Luther did not use the ballroom songs of his day...in fact he was extremely cautious in protecting the Word of God from any admixture of worldly elements." (p. 36 Leupold, U.S., Ed., *Luther's works; Liturgy and Hymns*, Fortress Press, 1965, as quoted by Dwight Gustafson, Should Sacred Music Swing? Faith for the family, Jan/Feb., 1975 p. 40.)

"Satan does not enter with his array of temptations at once. He disguises these temptations with a semblance of good; he mingles some little improvement with the folly and amusements...Satan's hellish arts are masked. Beguiled souls take one step, then are prepared for the next. It is much more pleasant to follow the inclinations of their own hearts than to stand on the defensive and resist the first insinuation of the wily foe, and thus shut out his incomings...Oh, what art, what skill, what cunning, is exercised to lead the professed followers of Christ to a union with the world by seeking for happiness in the amusements of the world, under the delusion that some good is to be gained!" (*Testimonies* Volume 2 page 142, 143)

"Death clad in the livery of heaven, lurks in the pathway of the young. Sin is gilded over by the church sanctity. These various forms of amusement in the churches of our day have ruined thousands who, but for them, might have remained upright and become the followers of Christ. Wrecks of character have been made by these fashionable church festivals and theatrical performances, and thousands more will be destroyed; yet people will not be aware of the danger, nor of the fearful influences exerted. Many young men and women have lost their souls through these corrupting influences." (Review & Herald, November 21, 1878)

*A mighty fortress is our God,*
*A bulwork never failing;*
*Our helper, He amid the flood*
*Of mortal ills prevailing.*

*For still our ancient foe*
*Doth seek to work us woe;*
*His craft and power are great;*
*And armed with cruel hate,*
*On earth is not his equal.*

*Did we in our own strength confide,*
*Our striving would be losing,*
*Were not the right man on our side,*
*The man of God's own choosing.*

*Dost ask who that may be?*
*Christ Jesus, it is He,*
*Lord Sabaoth His name,*
*From age to age the same,*
*And He must win the battle.*

And though this world, with devils filled,
Should threaten to undo us,
We will not fear, for God hath willed
His truth to triumph through us.

The prince of darkness grim,
We tremble not for Him;
His rage we can endure,
For lo! His doom is sure,
One little word shall fell him.

That word above all earthly powers,
No thanks to them, abideth;
The Spirit and the gifts are ours
Through Him who with us sideth;

Let goods and kindred go,
This mortal life also;
The body they may kill;
God's truth abideth still,
His kingdom is forever.

—Martin Luther

# 8

# When the Music Becomes the Messege

**Principle #3: When the beat overshadows the words, or the physical side of music takes precedence over the intellectual, the music is from beneath.**

Some people think Christians only like music without the rhythm. And indeed, from the comments some make, you would think that rhythm itself is wrong.

Nothing could be farther from the truth, however, for there is rhythm and rhyme throughout the entire universe. Every time the sun rises and sets, the tide ebbs and falls, or the earth follows its orbit around the sun, there is rhythm, order and predictability. Each breath you take, each pulse of your heart, even the cycles of the seasons, march to the beat of a natural rhythm.

But while there are natural rhythms that God built into our lives, some of the music we have today fights with those natural rhythms. Though these rhythms seem exciting or stimulating, our bodies are somehow disturbed by them. This is why fish die, sunflowers turn away, and rats become retarded and lose their way in a maze when exposed to certain subversive rhythms. As Christians, we can be sure that any music which causes such chaos in the world of nature attacks our own mental, physical and/or spiritual health as well.

In addition to the problem of unnatural rhythms, there is also the challenge of excessive or missing rhythm. It has been said that the rhythm of music is much like the rhythm of the heartbeat in the human body:

If there is no rhythm, the body is dead.

If there is the right speed and intensity of rhythm,
The body is healthy and wholesome.
If the rhythm is too powerful or fast, the body is sick.

When we translate this into the realm of music, we understand that:

Where there is no rhythm, the music is dead.
Where there is the right speed and intensity of rhythm,
The music is healthy and well, and
Where the rhythm is too fast or powerful, the music is sick.

Unfortunately, much of the popular music of our day features a strong overdose of rhythm. The television and movie industries spend millions, yes, billions of dollars to lure the youth into breaking down the principles of purity and destroying their bodies sexually. Satan is so subtle, the youth don't even realize when they've crossed the line. Soon they feel depressed and lose their desire for a life with Christ.

Satan takes advantage of the youthful mind to ensnare it into the use of body-destroying drugs and alcohol. Released from reality and unfettered by their God-given inhibitions, they soon find their consciences too broken to distinguish right from wrong. And sorry to say, much of this life-altering influence comes through the powerful medium of music.

Even Contemporary Christian Music (CCM), which is supposed to reach souls for Christ, is more often than not modeled after the destructive music of the world. In the words of one reporter:

"This wasn't sweet hour of prayer—this was rock and roll, sometimes soft and tender as the sweetest love song, sometimes hard edged and growling, but it wasn't words alone that brought the crowd clapping and cheering to their feet. There was some hefty assist for sing your praise from booming guitar lines and crashing drums."

As the last seconds of this earth's history tick into oblivion, the line between CCM and the music of the world is becoming increasingly difficult to distinguish.

"Youth night wasn't anything like I imagined," wrote a Tampa Bay high school sophomore who attended one of Billy Graham's evangelistic crusades for youth. "In some ways...it was like a regular rock concert. People danced in the stands and on the field. I was surprised to see girls dressed like hoochie mamas and teens smoking pot in the corner of the smoking balcony."

"I'm not a Christian, but these people seem happy," commented another teenager. "I'm an atheist. I don't believe in God, I'm here for the fun of it."

Perhaps it's the almighty dollar rather than a passion for savings souls, that is the driving force behind much of todays Contemporary Christian Music industry. And there is money to be had in this flourishing, multi-billion dollar enterprise: Successful CCM musicians sell thousands of any given album. That adds up to hundreds of thousands of dollars for each recording, and that is where the money is made.

CCM treats the message of salvation as just another product to be promoted. Phrases in CCM trade journals speak of "the gospel music industry," "the Jesus music scene," the "Christian market," and the "top twenty gospel hits." More than a few CCM entertainers split their time between churches and nightclubs. Perhaps their fans, who accept them in either place, haven't considered the following two texts:

"If you were of the world, the world would love his own..." (John 15:19)

"And through covetousness shall they with feigned words make merchandise of you..." (2 Peter 2:3)

Phil Wilson, a young man who played drums in rock groups for seven years before becoming a Christian, was encouraged by well-meaning friends to use his talents for the Lord. As a result, Phil formed a group to play what they considered to be "the new Christian sound."

"I thought our music, the length of our hair and the way we dressed would be more effective with young people," Phil said. Phil's group gave their testimonies with soft, slow music in the background, and when they gave the invitation to come forward, a hundred or more teenagers often responded.

At one point in his experience, however, Phil began to wonder how many of the conversions were really genuine. When he began to follow up on those who had come forward, he was shocked to find that almost everyone he could track had gone back to their old ways. Phil's group couldn't find one committed Christian they could consider to be the fruit of their ministry! In the end, Phil concluded that those who came forward were responding to the music, not the Holy Spirit. In other words, the power of the music had overridden the message to the point that the music, not the gospel, was the message.

Somehow, today, people want God to be an entertainer. And so they are busy dressing Him up to fit their lifestyle, whether it includes ragged jeans, unbuttoned shirts, or sensual dress. Unfortunately, we destroy the honor and reverence that is due to God when we present Him as a super star, clown, or worldly entertainer. This is a mockery. The church, as Christ's bride, should not belittle the bridegroom. Clowns, clothing and choreography are not needed to make the gospel appealing. Great men of faith have been martyrs, not swingers.

In society's continuing search for entertainment, we often forget that there was nothing entertaining about the eternal deity of Christ, bathed in the glory He had with His Heavenly Father "...before the world began." (John 17:5) There was nothing entertaining about His coming into the world and "...taking the very nature of a servant, being made in human likeness." (Philippians 2:7) There was nothing entertaining about His miracles; they were performed for "...God's glory so that God's Son could be glorified." (John 11:4) There was nothing entertaining about His life long struggle against temptation, "...for He suffered when He was tempted." (Hebrews 2:18) There was nothing entertaining about His prayer life, for we are told that "...He offered up prayers and petitions with loud cries and tears..." (Hebrews 5:7) There was nothing entertaining about His experience in the Garden of Gethsemane, when "... His sweat was like drops of blood falling to the ground." (Luke 22:44) There was nothing entertaining about His agonizing death on the cross, when the burden of our sin forced Him to cry out, "...My God, my God, why have you forsaken me?" (Matthew 27:46) There was nothing entertaining about His resurrection, by which He was "...declared with power to be the Son of God..."

(Romans 1:4)  There was nothing entertaining about His ascension into heaven, when He was "...taken up to Glory." (2 Timothy 3:16) There will be nothing entertaining when He returns to earth and "...every eye will see Him, even those who pierced Him..." (Revelation 1:7)  And there will be nothing entertaining when all of humanity stands before Him on the day of judgment and when as "...judge of the living and the dead." (Acts 10:42) He will pronounce the eternal destiny of every one of us.

The gospel is not a popular message, for the road is narrow that leads to eternal life, and few are they that find it.  In contrast, the wide road is easy and exciting, and the end thereof leads to death. Jesus Himself was despised of men.  He came to preach the straight truth—a truth that cuts to the core of sin and foolishness, leading us to repent and forsake sin.

Many young people think that if you draw a big crowd you are successful.  However, it's not the number of people that come to hear you sing but the quality, depth, and clarity of truth presented that is most important in witnessing.  The Seventh-day Adventist message is not the most popular message, but it is the truth for this time, and the one we are to proclaim.

We are not to judge our effectiveness by the number of churches or halls we can fill to overflowing.  We are to seek those who are honest in heart, to see how many hearts can be filled to overflowing by the Spirit of Christ through music and the spoken Word.

When we sugar-coat sin with questionable music, we show a false picture of the Christian life. The message of salvation is to be communicated by preaching. (1 Corinthians 1:21) Music should be secondary to the Word.  Yet many young people today want to be fed by music that preaches a partial gospel.  They don't hunger and thirst after righteousness, and they don't want sermons that cross their desires or bring them to full repentance.  Instead, they want music that excites the carnal nature and releases immoral desires, promoting false gods, ideas and doctrines.

More than a century ago, God's end-time prophetess foresaw these things.

"Eternal things have little weight with the youth," she wrote. "Angels of God are in tears as they write in the roll the words and acts

47

of professed Christians. Angels are hovering around yonder dwelling. The young are there assembled; there is the sound of vocal and instrumental music. Christians are gathered there, but what is that you hear? It is a song, frivolous ditty, fit for the dance hall. Behold the pure angels gather their light closer around them, and darkness envelops those in that dwelling. The angels are moving from the scene. Sadness is upon their countenances. Behold they are weeping. This I saw repeated a number of times all through the ranks of Sabbathkeepers...Music has occupied the hours which should have been devoted to prayer. Music is the idol which many professed Sabbathkeeping Christians worship. Satan has no objection to music if he can make that a channel through which to gain access to the minds of the youth. Anything will suit his purpose that will divert the mind from God and engage the time which should be devoted to His service. He works through the means which will exert the strongest influence to hold the largest numbers in a pleasing infatuation, while they are paralyzed by his power. When turned to a good account, music is a blessing; but it is often made one of Satan's most attractive agencies to ensnare souls. When abused, it leads the unconsecrated to pride, vanity, and folly. When allowed to take the place of devotion and prayer, it is a terrible curse. Young persons assemble to sing, and professed Christians, frequently dishonor God and their faith by their frivolous conversations and their choice of music. Sacred music is not congenial to their taste. I was directed to the plain teachings of God's word, which have been passed by unnoticed. In the judgment all these words of inspiration will condemn those who have not heeded them." (*Testimonies* Volume 1 page 505)

### Notable Quotes

The young people "...have a keen ear for music and Satan knows what organs to excite, to animate, engross and charm the mind so that Christ is not desired..." (*Adventist Home* page 407)

"A view of one such company was presented to me, where were assembled those who profess to believe the truth. One was seated at the instrument of music, and such songs were poured forth as made the angels weep. There was mirth, there was coarse laughter, there was abundance of enthusiasm, and a kind of inspiration; but the joy was such as Satan only is able to create. This is an enthusiasm and infatuation of which all who love God will be ashamed. It prepares the participants for unholy thought and action..." (*Adventist Home* page 514)

"If you lower the standard in order to secure popularity and an increase in numbers, and then make this increase a cause of rejoicing, you show great blindness. If numbers were an evidence of success, Satan might claim pre-eminence; for, in this world, his followers are largely in the majority. It is the degree of moral power pervading the college, that is the test of its prosperity. It is the virtue, intelligence and piety of the people composing our churches, not their numbers, that should be a source of joy and thankfulness." (*Christian Education* page 42)

Mrs. S.N. Haskell wrote Ellen White about a campmeeting in Muncie, Indiana, concerned about whether those things she had seen were indeed blessed by God. Here is Ellen White's answer to her letter. "...The things you have described as taking place in Indiana, the Lord has shown me would take place just before the close of probation. Every uncouth thing will be demonstrated. There will be shouting, with drums, music, and dancing. The senses of rational beings will become confused that they cannot be trusted to make right decisions. And this is called the moving of the Holy Spirit. The Holy Spirit never reveals itself in such methods, in such a bedlam of noise. This is an invention of Satan to cover up his ingenious methods for making of none effect the pure, sincere, elevating, ennobling, sanctifying truth for this time. Better never have the worship of God blended with music than to use musical instruments to do the work which last January was represented to me would be brought into our camp meetings. The truth for this time needs nothing of this kind in its work of converting souls. A bedlam of noise shocks the senses and perverts that which if conducted aright might be a blessing. The powers of Satan blend with the din and noise, to have a carnival, and this is termed the Holy Spirit's working." (*Selected Messages* Volume 2 page 36)

"Some minister's make the mistake of supposing that success depends on drawing a large congregation by outward display, and then delivering the message of truth in a theatrical style. But this is using common fire instead of the sacred fire of God's kindling. The Lord is not glorified by this manner of working..." (*Gospel Workers* page 383)

"...God would be better pleased to have six truly converted to the truth as a result of their labors, than to have sixty make a nominal profession, and yet not be thoroughly converted..." (*Evangelism* page 320)

*Sweet promise is given, to all who believe,*
*"Behold I come quickly, mine own to receive:*
*Hold fast till I come;*
*The danger is great;*
*Sleep not as do others;*
*Be watchful and wait.*

*Hold fast till I come, sweet promise of heaven—*
*"The kingdom restored, to you shall be given."*
*"Come, enter My joy,*
*Sit down on my throne;*
*Bright crowns are in waiting;*
*Hold fast till I come."*

—F.E. Belden

# 9

# Planting Your Feet on God's Word

**Principle #4:** We can trust God's Word to settle the music question for us.

Have you noticed most people are experts on music? Their analysis usually goes about as deep as (a) "I like it," (b) "I don't like it," or (c) "I get a blessing from it." This last argument is perhaps the most powerful of all, for it seems pretty hard-hearted to deny a soul the blessing they get from their music.

Since most of our minds are made up, we may not even want to hear about music anymore. It's impossible to study the Bible without hearing about music, however, for the Bible refers to this important topic more than five-hundred-fifty times. In fact, the Bible has more references to music than it does to heaven, hell, or even grace!

Imagine if a new pastor came to your church and said, "I hope you don't expect me to use the Bible, for I find it to be outdated. I think current philosophers and psychologists are much more relevant for today's generation."

No doubt your church wouldn't be too happy with this pastor, yet this is exactly what is happening in the field of music. We are more interested in pleasing the carnal nature than a "thus saith the Lord." Meanwhile, not many Adventists, even some of our highly educated musicians, have studied what the Bible says about music.

The deceptions of the Devil are pretty strong in these last days, and we need to be on our guard. If we would detect his counterfeits, we must be willing to "test the spirits" to see what is God's will and what is not.

"Testing the spirits" can be a little risky, for it may require a decision we don't really want to make. This reminds me of an experience we had with some friends in Glendale, California. My wife and I love Mexican food, and we often went to a popular Mexican restaurant with friends from our church. Being good vegetarians, we were shocked to hear one day that this restaurant had lard in their beans. We double-checked for ourselves, and found out the unhappy truth.

"I have bad news about the beans at the Mexican restaurant," my wife told our friends.

"Oh, don't tell us!" they quickly replied. "If we don't know, we can still eat there with a clear conscience."

If this is our attitude towards music, we should ask ourselves who we are fooling, God or ourselves? We need God's grace for wisdom, discernment, and the strength to make right decisions no matter how painful the truth may be.

In the words of the apostle John, "Beloved... test the spirits because many will come in My Name." (1 John 4:1) We can count on the Devil to work out numerous ways to influence our lives and try to keep us from God. But God has warned us to test it all, for not everything that comes in His name is really from Him. Though our choices appear "right" to us, if they don't agree with Scripture, the end of those choices might be something drastically different than we would like to admit. "There is a way that seems right to a man, but the end thereof is the way of death." (Proverbs 14:12)

The question we need to answer individually is whether we are willing to search the truth out for ourselves, "proving what is acceptable unto the Lord," (Ephesians 5:10 NAS) or are we content to follow the world in its taste for music and pleasure?

Part of the proving process involves hiding God's Word in your heart. This means to read it, digest it, and make it a part of our everyday lives. In the beautiful words of David, "I have hidden Your Word in mine heart, that I might not sin against You." (Psalms 119:11)

As you begin to ingest God's Word into your life, judgments that used to be very difficult for you will be easier than ever before. The choices will be obvious. When I was growing up, both my parents and minister really stressed the importance of personal daily devotions.

"You should read something out of God's Word every day," they would say. I didn't realize it then, but now I know that I could have avoided the traps of the Devil many times if I had read God's Word more. God's Word is to be the authoritative guide in every area of our lives, including music.

"All Scripture is inspired by God and profitable for teaching, for reproof, for correction, for training in righteousness." (II Timothy 3:16)

Music has the power to either build us up, or tear us down, spiritually. That is why it's so important for us to hold every song we sing up to the mirror of God's Word. "How can a young man keep his way pure? By guarding it according to Thy Word." (Psalms 119:9 NAS) That means we can make God's Scripture the basis for our choice. God's Word is dependable, for it is the "Sure Word." A tremendous burden is lifted from our shoulders when we rely on God to help us, rather than relying on our own tastes.

With God's help, we can be "proving what is acceptable to the Lord." (Ephesians 5:10) We can also recognize that God's Word applies to all areas of our life—regardless of our personal tastes or opinions. In the paraphrased words of Philippians 4:8:

"Finally, friends, whatever music is true, whatever music is honest, whatever music is just, whatever music is pure, whatever music is lovely, whatever music is of good report; if there be any virtue, and if there be any praise, listen to that music."

There are so many "flavors" of music today. Just when you think you've got it all figured out and have made a decision not to listen to a certain type of music, a new musical genre sneaks onto the scene. Then you have to go through the whole decision-making process all over again.

But though the Devil has done what he can to confuse the issue, God has given us His truth to guide us into right choices. In addition, "there must be a living connection with God in prayer, a living connection with God in songs of praise and thanksgiving," (Letter 96, 1898) if we are to make right choices.

In an age when flavors of popular music rise and wane too quickly to even keep up with, when people are tempted to explain away texts to justify their lifestyle, ease their conscience, or satisfy their personal desires, when accommodating theology is the norm rather than the exception, it's important for us to remember that "Jesus Christ is the same yesterday, today and forever." (Hebrews 13:8)

In an age when an increasing number of Adventists feel that the Spirit of Prophecy is out-of-date and written for the culture of the day, it is also important to remember that unfortunate attitudes and their unhappy consequences were, like so many events in Christian history, also foretold by the pen of a prophet:

"...Satan will work ingeniously, in different ways and through different agencies, to unsettle the confidence of God's remnant people in the true testimony." (*Selected Messages* Volume 1 page 48)

"The enemy has made his masterly efforts to unsettle the faith of our own people in the Testimonies...This is just as Satan designed it should be, and those who have been preparing the way for the people to pay no heed to the warnings and reproofs of the Testimonies of the Spirit of God will see that a tide of errors of all kinds will spring into life." (*Last Day Events* page 178)

"The very last deception of Satan will be to make of none effect the Testimony of the Spirit of God..." (*Last Day Events* page 177)

"Where there is no vision, the people perish..." (Proverbs 29:18)

### Notable Quotes:

"...There are few means more effective for fixing His words in the memory than repeating them in a song. And such song has wonderful power. It has power to subdue rude and uncultivated natures; power to quicken thought and to awaken sympathy, to promote harmony of action, and to banish the gloom and foreboding that destroy courage and weaken effort." (*Education* page 167, 168)

### Points to Ponder:

1) Have you ever been tempted to quote the Bible or Spirit of

Prophecy when they fit your theology, but ignore other passages that cross your cultural standards?

2) Do you believe in the Bible and Spirit of Prophecy as inspired words of instruction, relevant to our lives today?

3) If so, are you willing to accept what the Bible and Spirit of Prophecy teach about lifestyle issues-including music?

4) What do you think the above quotes should mean to you?

*Yes! This is our hope,*
*'Tis built on His word—*
*The glorious appearing of Jesus, our Lord;*
*Of promises all, it stands as the sun:*
*"Behold I come quickly, hold fast till I come."*

*"Hold fast till I come,"*
*Sweet promise of heaven—*
*"The kingdom restored,*
*To you shall be given."*

*"Come enter My joy,*
*Sit down on my throne;*
*Bright crowns are in waiting;*
*Hold fast till I come."*

—F.E. Belden

# 10

# The Trouble with Tainted Theology

**Principle #5: Just as a little poison spoils the stew, so a little error spoils the song.**

The devil is an expert at mixing teaspoons of error into buckets of truth. As a result, songs with "tainted theology" are one of the major music-related problems facing the Christian today. As Christians we have been instructed to love, think on, and sing about the truth. Yet many popular songs contain a perversion of truth, no matter how slight that perversion might be.

I am going to give you some examples in this chapter, and apply biblical principles to some songs that are either popular now, or have been in the past. In doing so I am not trying to "pick on" or focus on any particular singer. And, while this is only the tip of the iceberg, it should give you some ideas on how the Scripture can and should be applied to the words of various songs.

One song I heard sung repeatedly at our academies some years back was entitled "Grape Grape Joy" by Amy Grant. The lyrics start out innocently enough, or so it seems: "I am a small and lonely grape, clutching to the vine."

However, the next line seems to get into some murky theology to say the least, for this grape is "waiting for the day when I'll become my Savior's wine." Come to think of it, the Bible tells us that Jesus is the Vine and we are the branches, so we are not "grapes at all." His blood was shed for our sins, and is represented by the grape juice shared in communion services everywhere. And it is His blood, represented in the grape juice, we are to drink as a sign that we accept that blood in place of our sins.

The plot, or should I say, theological wine, thickens in the next few lines of the song, however. "Oh wouldn't French cuisine just yearn it, I've eternity to ferment..."

Let's hold the music just long enough to consider that heaven and eternity will be filled with abundant life, not fermentation. Also, our Lord was so set on keeping His mind clear at the cross that He refused a sponge soaked in vinegar (a fermented product), even when meant to relieve His pain. In the words of King Solomon, "...it is not for kings to drink wine; nor for princes strong drink: Lest they drink, and forget the law, and pervert the judgment of any of the afflicted." (Proverbs 31:4, 5)

But I'm not a king, you may be telling yourself. So this doesn't apply to me. But the book of Revelation tells us that Jesus "...hath made us kings and priests unto God and his Father; to Him be glory and dominion for ever and ever. Amen." (Revelation 1:6)

"Grape Grape Joy" is fun to sing, but whether or not a song is "fun" is not the most important question. The real question is "does this song build spirituality?"

Since it is theologically incorrect, making us His wine instead of His blood our wine, and winds up with the singer just "ripple in a cellar of chablais," the answer to that question would have to be a resounding "No!"

Another questionable song would be "You Light Up My Life," a song that was sung in many weddings and also applied in religious ways during the 1970's. The song has a beautiful melody and even more beautiful words—except for one problematic little line: "It can't be wrong, 'cause it feels so right..."

Hmmm....If Jesus had relied on His feelings, he would never have stayed on the cross. "...O my Father, if it be possible, let this cup pass from me,..." He agonized in the garden. In other words, He was less than enthusiastic about having nails driven through His tender flesh. But praise God, He did not act on His feelings. He acted out of principle, and this is the calling of every committed Christian.

And so we must ask ourselves the question, if I love the song "You Light up My Life," and listen to it over and over again, in spite of whatever good is wrapped into the words of the song, will the phrase "it can't be wrong, 'cause it feels so right," somehow worm its way into my psyche and undermine truth with error? If it does, we have a problem, for as Christians we have a responsibility to speak, and might I add sing, the truth.

Another very popular song that bothered me right from the start was Dallas Holm's "Rise Again." While the song is powerful and moving without a doubt, it seems to exalt a Christ who is not only defiant, but uses poor grammar.

*"Go ahead, drive the nails in my hands—*
*laugh at me, where you stand."*

This doesn't sound like turning the other cheek to me. Depending on how it is sung, it could even be termed as crucifixion trash talk, an incorrect image of Jesus taunting His persecutors!

*"...The day will come when you will see.*
*Cause I'll rise again—*
*ain't no power on earth can keep me down..."*

In other words, "I'll show you!" And so it goes. Yet, the Bible is clear. Christ didn't speak these words, or anything like them, when facing the cross. Read the story of the crucifixion, and you'll find an attitude of quiet submission. Our Savior had no defiant ego! (Matthew 26:39)

"He was oppressed and afflicted, yet He did not open His mouth; He was led like a lamb to the slaughter, and as a sheep before her shearers is silent, so He did not open His mouth." (Isaiah 53:7, NIV)

"Satan with his fierce temptations wrung the heart of Jesus. The Saviour could not see through the portals of the tomb. Hope did not present to Him, His coming forth from the grave a conqueror, or tell Him of the Father's acceptance of the sacrifice. He feared that sin was so offensive to God that Their separation was to be eternal. Christ felt the anguish which the sinner will feel when mercy shall no longer plead for the guilty race. It was the sense of sin, bringing the Father's wrath upon Him as man's substitute, that made the cup He drank so bitter, and broke the heart of the Son of God." (*Desire of Ages* page 753)

Jesus is not an egotistical God who says "go ahead—I will pay you back at the judgment!" No, He became very submissive out of His deep love for us. In His anguish, He even prayed "Father, forgive them, for they know not what they do," for those who hurt Him.

Many of today's popular Christian songs fail miserably in another important area: they do not promote a victorious Christian life.

"Now the works of the flesh are evident, which are: adultery, fornication, uncleanness, lewdness, idolatry, sorcery, hatred, contentions, jealousies, outbursts of wrath, selfish ambitions, dissension's, heresies, envy, murders, drunkenness, revelries, and the like; of which I tell you beforehand, just as I also told you in time past, that those who practice such things will not inherit the kingdom of God. But the fruit of the Spirit is love, joy, peace, longsuffering, kindness, goodness, faithful- ness, gentleness, self-control. Against such there is no law. And those who are Christ's have crucified the flesh with its passions and desires. If we live in the Spirit, let us also walk in the Spirit. Let us not become conceited, provoking one another, envying one another." (Galatians 5:19-26, NKJV)

This verse describes the works of the flesh, the fruits of evil you come out of when you become a Christian. If your music is centered on these works of the flesh (e.g. slander, envy, strife, carousing, and spirits that contradict what Christ wants to do with us), there is a problem.

Christ-centered music should fill us with peace and compassion. It should make us long-suffering and fill us with joy. If music puts you in a carousing mood, a mood to engage in sensual, worldly feelings, look out! The chapter we just quoted from above, Galations 5, is very explicit about these things and we should test our music by this text.

"For the sinful nature desires what is contrary to the Spirit, and the Spirit what is contrary to the sinful. They are in conflict with each other, so that you do not what you want." (Galatians 5:17)

This reminds me of another one of Amy Grant's songs, "I Have Decided." This song speaks of trying to be good, but always falling back to the old self. The message of this song is that Jesus doesn't really care what you do. As long as you accept Him, you won't have to be concerned about victorious Christian living.

Now I leave it for you to decide: which side of Galations 5 does "I Have Decided" fall on?

Another Amy Grant song seems to be talking about Baby Jesus. "Baby, baby, I'm taken with the notion to love you with the sweetest devotion," the song begins. "Baby, Baby my tender love will flow from the bluest sky to the deepest ocean. Stop for a minute; baby I'm so glad you're mine yeah, you're mine."

Test this song by Scripture, and I believe you will find that the entire song degrades the dignity and love of God, bringing Him down to a human level. Making God into what we want Him to be, rather than being the children He wants us to be, is a real temptation to we humans. While Amy's song speaks of two people loving each other, they are on an equal plane. However, bringing God down to our level certainly can't be the New Song He promised us when we come to Him.

Let us test one more song and see what you think.

*Dear Lord and Father of mankind,*
*Forgive our foolish ways;*
*Reclothe us in our rightful mind,*
*In purer lives Thy service find,*
*In deeper reverence praise,*
*In deeper reverence praise.*

*Breathe thro' the heats of our desire,*
*Thy coolness and Thy balm;*
*Let sense be dumb, let flesh retire,*
*Speak thro' the earthquake, wind, and fire,*
*O still small voice of calm,*
*O still small voice of calm.*

Here we find God as our hope. Through this hymn, we may reverently ask God to control our desires and speak to us through His still, small voice. What a contrast between this hymn and Amy Grant's song, which turns God into some sort of a human "buddy." One song is a love song that could be sung to anyone, the other seeks forgiveness and God's assistance to help us control our desires and live purer lives.

### Notable Quotes:

"As I was pleading with a young man to turn to the Savior, he said: 'I am not ready. This band of music would be broken up should I leave it. I am needed in this circle of society. And besides, I want my liberty.' But he did not know of what he was talking. There is no liberty save that which is brought to us by Christ. We can find in sin nothing but slavery..." (Youth's Instructor August 21, 1902)

*I would be true, for there are those who trust me;*
*I would be pure, for there are those who care;*
*I would be strong, for there is much to suffer;*
*I would be brave; for there is much to dare*

—Howard Arnold Walter

# 11

# Will You Stand on the Plain of Dura?

**Principle #6:** As children of God, we need to be listening to His music as we grow into His image.

**Principle #7:** God is looking for Christians who will stand "on the plain of Dura," refusing to succumb to Satan's temptations, bow down to his image, or listen to his music.

Few showdowns in Bible history were as pivotal as the incident between Nebuchadnezzar, and the three Hebrew worthies on the Plain of Dura. There we find three young men willing to stand, and even die, for what they believed rather than bow to the golden image.

Their answer to the king in this hour of decision is instructive for all of us: "O Nebuchadnezzar, we do not need to defend ourselves before you in this matter. If we are thrown into the blazing furnace, the God we serve is able to save us from it, and He will rescue us from your hand, O king. But even if He does not, we want you to know, O king, that we will not serve your gods or worship the image of gold you have set up." (Daniel 3:16-18)

What a commitment to the only true God! These men were simply not willing to bow, no matter what the cost.

As "enlightened" Christians today, we like to think we would never bow down to a golden image. Yet we have many idols, designer gods that bend to our personal wants, perspectives and personalities. Even music itself has become a god to many. It is an image they bow to even though it puts man's image in place of God's, thus taking away true worship.

Whether we realize it or not, we are standing on a plain today—the musical Plain of Dura. Like the three Hebrew worthies so long ago, we have a decision to make, whether to stand or bow. And there are questions we should ask as we ponder this decision, soul-searching, heart-wrenching questions. They are difficult ones, but they must be asked if you are to remain standing, no matter how loud the music plays, on the end-time Plain of Dura.

Who is your God?
Is he made in *your* image,
designed to satisfy *your* needs
without crossing *your* desires?

Does your god fulfill *your* wants
At the snap of a finger
Is "he" a genie in a bottle
to be "called" at any time?

Is your god a "designer god"
planned to fit the mold you choose?
Or were you made in *His* image
Designed to glorify His name?

Are your heart's desires met
As you do *His* precious will.
Is your god a "designer god"-
Planned to fit your own perspective,

Or is he *the* Designer God
Maker of the Universe
King of all creation and
Ruler of your heart?

In case you've missed it, "designer gods" are fabricated from *our* feelings, baked in the ovens of *our* desire, fired in the kiln of *our* imagination, a god worshipped for what He can do for us.

Such a concept of God is no less heathen than the golden image erected by Nebuchadnezzar on the Plain of Dura.

If your god:

- stands idly by while you cheat on your business
- smiles benignly at teenage foolishness
- laughs at your lurid remarks
- makes excuses for x-rated movies
- pats you on the back as you contemplate an affair
- looks the other way when you indulge in destroying your body with alcohol, drugs or poor diet
- allows you to abuse your wife
- makes no demands, asks no favors, and closes no doors to worldly desires,

Then your god is 'a designer god,' a heathen god fabricated by your own feelings and conditioned by culture. The fact that you call him God, or even Jesus, makes Him no different than a statue on the Plain of Dura.

So please, don't accept designer doctrines, fabricated in the New Age laboratories of our heathen society. Don't play church with a religion made in your own image, an image that makes no demands on you or your life. Such religion bears no resemblance to the religion of Jesus Christ, for He told us not to divorce, judge others, swear or defend yourself in court. Instead, we are admonished to turn the other cheek, give to those who ask, love our enemies and resist evil persons.

This is no mealy-mouthed religion we're talking about here, a designer religion that scratches your back when you turn in your tithe. This is a call to heroism. It is a counter-culture movement that cannot and will not tolerate 'designer gods' fabricated in the moral furnace of Hollywood.

With the three Hebrew children, true Christians will tell the kings of this world that even if our God does not save us, "we want you to know, O king that we will not serve your gods or worship the image of gold you have set up."

In other words, we will not bow down to your counterfeits

whether they involve false worship, a false day of worship, an unhealthy diet or no diet at all. And we will not listen to your music.*

*Many of the thoughts from this article were taken from an excellent sermon presented by Dr. Gordon Bietz, president of Southern Adventist University, entitled "Will You Stand Up When You Come to the Plain of Dura?"*

*Standing by a purpose true,*
*heeding God's command,*
*Honor them the faithful few,*
*all hail to Daniels band!*
*Dare to be a Daniel,*
*Dare to stand alone!*
*Dare to have a purpose firm!*
*Dare to make it known*

—P. P. Bliss

# 12

# Sing a "New Song" to the Lord

**Principle #8:** The music of Christ will not be the same as the world's.

**Principle #9:** If we come to Jesus and surrender to Him just as we are, He will change our tastes in music.

Every single gift God blesses us with is designed to bring us to the point where we can praise Him forever. He wants to change us and make us new people! Some of these gifts are spiritual like the ones listed in Ephesians 4:11-16.

Spiritual gifts should edify the body of Christ, build the saints to spiritual maturity and equip them for ministry. These are the distinguishing marks of the Christian.

"Every good gift and every perfect gift is from above, and cometh down from the Father of lights, with whom is no variableness, neither shadow of turning." (James 1:17) If the music we listen to doesn't build us towards maturity in Christ, it is not a spiritual tool sent from God. It's that simple.

Although everybody seems to have a different idea of what worldliness means these days, God's Word says exactly what it means.

"Pure religion and undefiled before God and the Father is this, to visit the fatherless and widows in their affliction, and to keep himself unspotted from the world." (James 1:27)

Did you catch that last phrase?

"Don't be stained or spotted with the world," God tells us. "When somebody looks at you, or is with you when you do a certain activity, they should not see the stain of the world upon you."

Here is another great text:

"Love not the world, neither the things that are in the world. If any man love the world, the love of the Father is not in him. For all that is in the world, the lust of the flesh, and the lust of the eyes, and the pride of life, is not of the Father, but is of the world. And the world passeth away, and the lust thereof: but he that doeth the will of God abideth for ever." (1 John 2:15-17)

In other words, don't love the things of the world because they are not compatible with things of the Spirit, the things of God. If the music we are listening to, either the music itself, or the lyrics, is patterned after the same things the world has to offer, then there is a problem.

I am continually reminded of Psalm 40:3:

"He hath put a *new song* in my mouth, even praise unto our God: many shall see it, and fear, and shall trust in the LORD."

It's a new song! A different type of music, different than what we have had before. So it cannot be the same as the world's.

Music changes people and it will change us when we listen to it and make it a part of us. As a result, many times we can tell if music is good or bad simply by watching the effect it has on others.

The Bible tells us that he "...who is wise and under-standing...(will) show by his good behavior his deeds in the gentleness of wisdom." (James 3:13, NAS) In addition, "the seed whose fruit is righteousness is sown in peace by those who make peace." (James 3:18, NAS) "Ye shall know them by their fruits..." (Matthew 7:16-20)

So it will be very easy to tell by the way professed Christian musicians live, act and carry themselves if what they are singing about really is inside. If it is not what's really inside, then they have a different purpose for their music and we had better beware.

"For the sinful nature desires what is contrary to the Spirit, and the Spirit what is contrary to the sinful. They are in conflict with each other, so that you do not do what you want." (Galations 5:17, NIV)

That's why combining holy words with worldly music is a contradiction. When religious words are combined with rock, it completely undercuts the message of the lyrics.

Unfortunately, much of today's contemporary Christian music relies on the same flavor of background beat, instrumentation, arranging and sound as the music of the world. Yet somehow the religious lyrics are expected to turn this wordly music into a sacred song.

Although much of the Christian world doesn't seem to understand the incongruity between rock and the gospel, the secular entertainers on Saturday Night Live certainly do. As you probably know, nothing is sacred on Saturday Night Live. They have commercials that poke fun at other commercials, and little snapshots of TV shows that make fun of other TV shows.

Several years ago, in a skit entitled "Jesus in Blue Jeans," they poked fun at the very idea of religious rock music with a bogus ad that read something like this:

"Parents, are you troubled by the moral decay rampant among today's teenagers? Have you ever wondered what your young people are listening to on those tiny phones of theirs? I can assure you it's not our Master's voice. No sir, it's the secret stereophonic whisperings of Satan. How many times have we seen a youngster listen to a rock and roll recording and then talk back to his parents and fornicate..."

"Never forget it's only a short skip from the phonograph needle to the hypodermic needle. Rock and roll music is the Devil's music, until now. Because for just $9.98 (man holding up record with Jesus dressed in blue jeans) you can use this same music to deliver your children from evil. It's all here in my new born again rock and roll collection—"Jesus in Blue Jeans."

Get twenty-four rock hits, but no sex and no drugs. Just good rock and love songs to God. Here is just some of what you get: (music in background... "Help me Jesus, Help, Help Me Jesus") These are great rock and roll classics. (more music..."It's My Party, and I Will Pray if I Want to, You Would Pray Too if it Happened to You") ("The Messiah is Back, The Messiah is Back and There's Gonna Be Trouble, hey la, hey la. Satan is Here You Better Cut Out on The Double, hey la, hey la.") And how about my personal favorite. (music in background...."Yummy, Yummy, Yummy, I've Got God in My Tummy, And I Feel Like Loving Him." In the background is a picture of the last supper.) You can get this great Christmas classic (music in background..."Baby Lord, My Baby Lord, I Need You,

O How I Need Love") Ah my Lord, That's righteous music."
And so it went. Actually there was quite a bit more, but it was
so blasphemous I would rather not repeat it. It is interesting to note
that Saturday Night Live, a truly secular company whose only intent is
making more money, recognized in this ad the incongruitiy of Christians listening to rock and roll set to religious words. They don't even
think there should be a connection, which is why they made fun of the
very idea.

Scripture shows us very clearly that there are old habits and new
habits. These represent the differences between the old man and the
new man, the old life and the new life. There are several excellent
references we can point to for that.

"That in reference to your former manner of life, you lay aside
the old self, which is being corrupted in accordance with the lusts of
deceit, and that you be renewed in the spirit of your mind, and put on
the new self, which in the likeness of God has been created in righteousness and holiness of the truth." (Ephesians 4:22-24, NAS)

"If then you have been raised up with Christ, keep seeking the
things above, where Christ is, seated at the right hand of God. Set
your mind on things above, not on the things that are on earth. For you
have died and your life is hidden with Christ in God. When Christ,
who is our life, is revealed, then you also will be revealed with Him in
glory." (Colossians 3:1-4, NAS)

"What shall we say then? Are we to continue in sin that grace
might increase? May it never be! How shall we who died to sin still
live in it? Or do you not know that all of us that have been baptized
into Christ Jesus have been baptized into His death? Therefore we
have been buried with Him through baptism into death, in order that
as Christ was raised from the dead through the glory of the Father, so
we too might walk in newness of life." (Romans 6:1-4, NAS)

"But I say, walk by the Spirit, and you will not carry out the
desire of the flesh. For the flesh sets its desire against the Spirit, and
the Spirit against the flesh; for these are in opposition to one another,
so that you may not do the things that you please." (Galations 5:16-17,
NAS)

"You adulteresses, do you not know that friendship with the
world is hostility toward God? Therefore whoever wishes to be a

friend of the world makes himself an enemy of God." (James 4:4, NAS)

The texts show the tension between what is our natural bent in life, and what Christ wants to do for us. The things of the old life are not compatible with the new life. They simply can't work together.

James 4 and 1 John 2 say more of the same—that friendship with the world puts you at odds with Christ. You can't hang on to both. They are not compatible, and trying to hang on to the world actually puts you at opposition to Christ.

So what should we do if, like so many others, we have been listening to the music of the world? First of all, it's important to know that we can depend on God to change our tastes. We don't have to worry about it!

Sometimes young people get so discouraged. They know what God wants them to do, yet it's difficult to change. And they don't know what to do, for they feel they must change completely before God will hear their prayers.

If such is the case with you, I would recommend an old song I used to love as a teenager. I responded once myself to Jesus, and asked Him to take me just as I was. And that old hymn, 'Just As I Am,' told me that Jesus would!

"Don't worry, children," He says to us. "I've paid the price! I've paid it for you, and you're mine. So come as you are, today. Listen to His sweet invitation, in the beautiful words of this song:

*Just as I am, without one plea*
*But that Thy blood was shed for me.*
*And that Thou bid'st me come to Thee,*
*O Lamb of God, I come, I come.*

*Just as I am, Thou wilt receive,*
*Wilt welcome, pardon, cleanse, relieve;*
*Because Thy promise I believe,*
*O Lamb of God, I come, I come.*

*—written by Charlotte Elliott*

## Notable Quotes:

"Conformity to worldly customs converts the church to the world; it never converts the world to Christ. Familiarity with sin will inevitably cause it to appear less repulsive..." (*Great Controversy* page 509)

# 13

# Judging Each Other's Song

**Principle #10: Our job is to judge music, not people.**

**Principle #11: We are not to give up on God's children, for many who seem to have little or no spiritual potential will be truly converted and become ardent workers in God's cause.**

As I've held Weeks of Prayer from time to time, I've met many young people who were concerned about the music in their lives. Sometimes they even wonder if Jesus can still love them, after the things they've been listening to. And it is important to remember that God does love us all, no matter what kind of music we have been listening to. At the same time, however, God wants our lives to reflect more of His life as we get to know Him better. He has also promised that He would give us that "new song."

We should not judge these young people, for God's mercy is still open to receive, and the opportunity to forsake our sin is available right now.

"These souls whom you despise as worthless, said Jesus, are the property of God. They are his by creation and by redemption, and they are of value in his sight. They are the objects of his care and love. As the shepherd loves his sheep, and cannot rest if one be missing, so, in an infinitely higher degree, does God love every outcast and wandering soul. Men may deny the claim of his love, they may wander far from him, they may choose for themselves another master, yet are they God's, and he longs to recover his own. And he says, As a shepherd seeketh out his flock in the day that he is among his sheep that are scattered; so will I seek out my sheep, and will deliver them out of all places where they have been scattered in the cloudy and dark day." (Ezekiel 34:12)

"O soul lost in sin, however far you have wandered, into whatever depths of degradation and misery you have sunken, God recognizes you as his own, precious to His heart of love. You cannot be safe or happy without Him, and He cannot be satisfied without you. Amid the angels that surround the throne, He still yearns to recover you." (General Conference Bulletin, December 1, 1895)

As Christians we ought to be very careful about judging someone else's song. We need to set our own hearts in tune with Jesus. The closer our relationship becomes to Him the more pure will be the song He can give us. So we must, on an individual basis, choose what we are going to do for the Lord in music.

Because our youth are under great pressure, we need to love them and be patient with them. We must understand that there are many voices to listen to, and these voices make it difficult to choose what is God's and what is counterfeit. We have great young people who will rise up to be faithful to follow God's leading in their lives. God is putting His hand on those with whom we are sometimes impatient.

"...Often those whom we pass by with indifference because we judge them from outward appearance, have in them the best materials for workers and will repay all the efforts bestowed on them..." (*Gospel Workers* p. 208)

Let us worry about our own house being in order first. Even then we must not judge others by our standards. We must test the standard by Scripture and the inspired writings to the church. Let us pray not for people to come up to our standard, but to God's standard, which all are still striving to reach. There may be music programs we are not comfortable in participating in, and our absence may be giving a message, but our tongue can ruin all the good that could have been done. My prayer is that all God's children may reach the high standard He would have us reach.

## Notable Quotes:

"...When we reach the standard that the Lord would have us reach, worldlings will regard Seventh-day Adventists as odd, singular, strait-laced extremists...." (*Fundamentals of Christian Education* page 289)

# 14

# The Devil's Primary Target

**Principle #12: While music is one of the greatest blessings given by God, it is also one of Satan's primary tools to ensnare the young.**

I was preaching one Sabbath at a college church, and after the service I was stopped by a man who related this story:

"Two years ago you were at our campmeeting giving a seminar on music. I left in disgust when you talked about the influence of rock music on young people. My boys were in their early teens at the time, and my wife and I were also involved in rock music, and didn't see the evil influence. It gave us an exhilarating feeling, and an escape from our problems. Now two years later I'm coming to ask you to pray for my boys for they have left home, and are into drugs and rock to the point that I fear for their lives. My wife and I have since stopped our habit of listening to rock and renewed an active relationship with the church. I'm happy to say we are strong in the Lord again."

Throughout my youth ministry this story has been repeated many times. I assured him that God has not given up on his children, and shared a statement from the Spirit of Prophecy that has meant a great deal to me concerning my own children:

"The love of God still yearns over the one who has chosen to separate from Him, and He sets in operation influences to bring him back to the Father's house..." (*Christ's Object Lessons* page 202)

What a wonderful assurance that God loves us so much that He continually strives with all of us when we stray. Let us not sit in judgment about our youth, rather, let us be in prayer for them. Please consider the words of inspiration given to our church concerning youth and music. "How can I endure the thought that most of the youth in this age will come short of everlasting life: Oh that the sound of instrumental music might cease and they no more while away so much precious time in pleasing their own fancy..." (*Testimonies* Volume 2 page 144)

It would seem to me that there should be an alarm sounding in the ears of all who are parents. In the words of the apostle John, "I have no greater joy than to hear that my children walk in truth." (III John 4) This is the prayer of all parents, but notice how the evil one comes to tempt our children.

"...I feel alarmed as I witness everywhere the frivolity of young men and women who profess to believe the truth. God does not seem to be in their thoughts. Their minds are filled with nonsense. Their conversation is only empty, vain talk. They have a keen ear for music, and Satan knows what organs to excite to animate, engross, and charm the mind so that Christ is not desired. The spiritual longings of the soul for divine knowledge, for a growth in grace, are wanting. I was shown that the youth must take a higher stand and make the word of God the man of their counsel and their guide. Solemn responsibilities rest upon the young, which they lightly regard. The introduction of music into their homes, instead of inciting to holiness and spirituality, has been the means of diverting their minds from the truth. Frivolous songs and the popular sheet music of the day seem congenial to their taste. The instruments of music have taken time which should have been devoted to prayer. Music, when not abused, is a great blessing; but when put to a wrong use, it is a terrible curse. It excites, but does not impart that strength and courage which the Christian can find only at the throne of grace while humbly making known his wants and with strong cries and tears pleading for heavenly strength to be fortified against the powerful temptations of the evil one. Satan is leading the young captive..." (Testimonies Volume 1 pages 496-497)

Elder James White showed great concern about music and youth, and spoke about it during a sermon he preached in Battle Creek in 1869.

"There are those in whose hearts has been inspired an extreme love of worldly amusements. Singing is not to be objected to by any means, if held subordinate to the principles of religion. Would to God that we all sung. But it has been turned to a bad account. And then various other amusements have been advocated as being healthful, innocent, and even necessary. It has been stated that if you take them away from the young, there would be a vacancy which nothing else could fill, and they would run to ruin. This is of the Devil's arguments." (Sermon by James White, February 13, 1869, R & H March 16, 1869)

Satan is going about as a roaring lion in these last days, seeking whom he may devour. One of his primary targets is the young, and one of his primary tools in ensnaring the young is music.

The Devil uses his fleshly music to appeal to the lower passions and ruin the lives of young people. But praise God, the Creator also uses music as a powerful tool to save souls. This tool, especially when rightly used, is powerful in the hands of the youth. And this is why the Devil works so hard to deceive them. The following quote has already been included earlier in this book, yet I think it is so important it bears repeating:

"Eternal things have little weight with the youth. Angels of God are in tears as they write in the roll the words and acts of professed Christians. Angels are hovering around yonder dwelling. The young are there assembled; there is the sound of vocal and instrumental music. Christians are gathered there, but what is that you hear? It is a song, frivolous ditty, fit for the dance hall. Behold the pure angels gather their light closer around them, and darkness envelops those in that dwelling. The angels are moving from the scene. Sadness is upon their countenances. Behold they are weeping. This I saw repeated a number of times all through the ranks of Sabbathkeepers.....Music has occupied the hours which should have been devoted to prayer. Music is the idol which many professed Sabbathkeeping Christians worship. Satan has no objection to music if he can make that a channel through which to gain access to the minds of the youth. Anything will suit his purpose that will divert the mind from God and engage the time which should be devoted to His service. He works through the means which will exert the strongest influence to hold the largest numbers in a pleasing infatuation, while they are paralyzed by his power. When turned to a good account, music is a blessing; but it is often made one of Satan's most attractive agencies to ensnare souls. When abused, it leads the unconsecrated to pride, vanity, and folly. When allowed to take the place of devotion and prayer, it is a terrible curse. Young persons assemble to sing, and although professed Christians, frequently dishonor God and their faith by their frivolous conversations and their choice of music. Sacred music is not congenial to their taste. I was directed to the plain teachings of God's Word, which have been passed by unnoticed. In the judgment all these words of inspiration will condemn those who have not heeded them." (*Testimonies* Volume 1 page 505, 506)

### *Notable Quotes:*

"Satan is continually seeking to overcome the people of God by breaking down the barriers which separate them from the world..." (*Great Controversy* page 508)

"Conformity to worldly customs converts the church to the world; It never converts the world to Christ. Familiarity with sin will inevitably cause it to appear less repulsive..." (*Great Controversy* page 509)

"Let none suppose that they can live a life of selfishness, and then, having served their own interest, enter into the joy of their Lord. In the joy of unselfish love they could not participate. They would not be fitted for the heavenly courts. They could not appreciate the pure atmosphere of love that pervades heaven. The voices of the angels and the music of their harps would not satisfy them. To their minds the science of heaven would be an enigma." (*Christ's Object Lessons* pages 364-365)

"I waited patiently for the Lord; he turned to me and heard my cry. He lifted me out of the slimy pit, out of the mud and mire; he set my feet on a rock and gave me a firm place to stand. He put a new song in my mouth, a hymn of praise to our God. Many will see and fear and put their trust in the Lord." (Psalm 40:1-3, NIV)

# 15

# The Beauty of Soft and Simple

**Principle #13: Music can be a powerful witnessing tool in the hands of dedicated Christian youth.**

Music played a large role in the work of the many youth witnessing teams I have directed over the years. Each of these teams chose not to use the electrical instruments and drums. Although I believe these instruments could have been used to the glory of God, they are closely associated with the rock beat which breaks down respect for parents, country, and God. We did use guitars, however, for a guitar played for God's glory by a dedicated young person can be a truly beautiful instrument.

Our youth witnessing teams always tried, in their music, to exemplify the gentle, kind, and meek spirit of our Savior. We also tried to lead the youth to uphold the standards of, and respect for, our church through their music. In doing this work, we were only following the inspired counsel of Ellen G. White:

"Students (youth) go out into the highways and hedges. Endeavor to reach the higher as well as the lower classes. Enter the homes of the rich and the poor, and as you have opportunity ask would you be pleased to have us sing? We should be glad to hold a song service with you. Then as hearts are softened, the way may open for you to offer a few words of prayer for the blessing of God. Not many will refuse." (Review & Herald August 27, 1903)

One youth witnessing experience that really stands out in my mind involved an alcoholic who also happened to be a millionaire. A pastor had asked us to witness to this lady, and when we arrived at her home, she welcomed us with a smile.

One of the young men introduced the team and told her we had just come to sing a few songs to her. As the team began to sing some of the simple, familiar hymns, she began to weep and we knew the Holy Spirit was working on her heart. After about the third song some of the youth testified of their experience with Christ, and this, too, made a deep impression on her.

After a few more songs, she stood up and pointed to a picture on the wall.

"That is a picture of my father," she told us. "He was brought up a Catholic, and was known for his honesty." She went on to tell us how, at one point in his life, her father had purchased a Bible and studied it for himself. As he studied, he became convinced that Saturday was the true day of worship. And so he kept the Sabbath for the rest of his life.

"I know you young people keep the right day," she told us, and began to weep again.

"May we pray with you?" asked one of the young ladies from our team.

"I would love that," she answered.

This witness opened the way for further contact and study by the pastor. It also gave our youth team a stronger faith in the promises of the wonderful Spirit-led writings of Ellen White.

As one who has been involved in many of these types of experiences, I can say with conviction that it's not the beauty of form, or ceremonies, or dress, or even accomplishment, that God can use best, but the willing heart and simple voice that sings with understanding.

We also tried to follow the inspired counsel when choosing the songs to sing. Following are some of the guiding principles I have found most helpful in this regard:

**Principle #14: God's music can be very effective in helping us to encourage others, resist temptation, and memorize Scripture.**

"It (music) is one of the most effective means of impressing the heart with spiritual truth. How often to the soul hard-pressed and ready to despair, memory recalls some word of God's, the long forgotten burden of a childhood song, and temptations lose their power, and life takes on new meaning and new purpose, and courage, and gladness are imparted to other souls!" (*Education* page 168)

"Song is a weapon that we can always use against discouragement. As we thus open the heart to the sunlight of the Saviour's presence, we shall have health and His blessing." (*Ministry of Healing* page 254)

"As the people journeyed through the wilderness, many precious lessons were fixed in their minds by means of song. At their deliverance from Pharaoh's army the whole host of Israel had joined in the song of triumph. Far over desert and sea rang the joyous refrain, and the mountains re-echoed the accents of praise, "Sing ye to the Lord, for He hath triumphed gloriously" (Exodus 15:21). Often on the journey was this song repeated, cheering the hearts and kindling the faith of the pilgrim travelers. The commandments as given from Sinai, with promises of God's favor and records of His wonderful works for their deliverance, were by divine direction expressed in song, and were chanted to the sound of instrumental music, the people keeping step as their voices united in praise." (*Education* page 39)

"There must be a living connection with God in prayer, a living connection with God in songs of praise and thanksgiving." (Letter 96, 1898)

**Principle #15: Even simple songs, when sung to the glory of God, may touch the hearts of others and win them to Christ.**

"Learn to sing the simplest of songs. These will help you in house to house labor, and hearts will be touched by the influence of the Holy Spirit." (Review & Herald August 27, 1903)

"...The melody of song, poured forth from many hearts in clear distinct utterance, is one of God's instrumentality's in the work of saving souls..." (*Testimonies* Volume 5 page 493)

"Song is one of the most effective means of impressing spiritual truth upon the heart. Often by the words of sacred song, the springs of penitence and faith have been unsealed." (Review & Herald June 6, 1912)

"The conversion of souls to God is the greatest work, the highest work, in which human beings can have a part. In the conversion of souls God's forbearance, His unbounded love, His holiness, His power, are revealed. Every true conversion glorifies Him, and causes the angels to break forth into singing..." (*Evangelism* page 292)

"...The soul redeemed and cleansed from sin, with all its noble powers dedicated to the service of God, is of surpassing worth; and there is joy in heaven in the presence of God and the holy angels over one soul redeemed, a joy that is expressed in songs of holy triumph." (*Steps to Christ* page 126)

**Principle #16: It is not loud singing that is needed, but soft, silvery tones. We should train our voices to sing in this heavenly manner.**

"Great improvement can be made in singing. Some think that the louder they sing the more music they make; but noise is not music. Good singing is like the music of the birds—subdued and melodious." (*Evangelism* page 510)

"I have often been pained to hear untrained voices, pitched to the highest key, literally shrieking the sacred words of some hymn of praise. How inappropriate those sharp, rasping voices for the solemn, joyous worship of God. I long to stop my ears, or flee from the place, and I rejoice when the painful exercise is ended." (*Evangelism* page 507)

"...It is not loud singing that is needed, but clear intonation, correct pronunciation and distinct utterance. Let all take time to cultivate the voice, so that God's praise can be sung in clear, soft tones, not with harshness and shrillness that offended the ear..." (*Testimonies* Volume 9 page 144)

"Your voice has been heard in church so loud, so harsh, accompanied or set off with your gesticulations not the most graceful, that the softer and more silvery strains, more like angel music, could not be heard. You have sung more to men than to God. As your voice has been elevated in loud strains above all the congregation, you have been thoughtful of the admiration you were exciting. You have really had such high ideas of your singing, that you have had some thoughts that you should be remunerated for the exercise of this gift." (*Selected Messages* Volume 3 page 335)

"This bodily exercise and the harsh, loud voice makes no melody to those who hear on earth and those who listen in heaven. This singing is defective and not acceptable to God as perfect, softened, sweet strains of music. There are no such exhibitions among the angels as I have sometimes seen in our meetings. Such harsh notes and gesticulations are not exhibited among the angel choir. Their singing does not grate upon the ear. It is soft and melodious and comes without this great effort I have witnessed. It is not forced and strained, requiring physical exercise." (*Selected Messages* Volume 3 page 333)

**Principle #17: God wants us to sing with the spirit and understanding, and when we do, the angels will join our song.**

"Singing with the spirit and understanding also is a great addition to devotional services in the house of God." (*Selected Messages* Volume 3 page 335)

"I saw that all should sing with the Spirit and understanding also." (*Testimonies* Volume 1 page 146)

"Many are singing beautiful songs in the meetings, songs of what they will do, and what they mean to do; but some do not do these things; they do not sing with the spirit and the understanding also. So in the reading of the Word of God, some are not benefited, because they do not take it into their very life, they do not practice it." (Review and Herald, Sept. 27, 1892)

"…no words can properly set forth the deep blessedness of genuine worship. When human beings sing with the Spirit and the understanding, heavenly musicians take up the strain, and join in the song of thanksgiving…" (*Testimonies* Volume 9 page 143)

**Principle #18: The nearer Christ's people come to correct, harmonious singing, the more God is glorified, the church is blessed, and unbelievers will be favorably impressed.**

"…God is not pleased with jargon and discord. Right is always more pleasing to Him than wrong, and the nearer the people of God can approach to correct, harmonious singing the more is

He glorified, and the church benefited, and unbelievers favorably affected." (*Testimonies* Volume 1 page 146)

"Gorgeous apparel, fine singing, and instrumental music in the church do not call forth the songs of the angel choir. In the sight of God these things are like the branches of the unfruitful fig tree which bore nothing but pretentious leaves. Christ looks for fruit, for principles of goodness and sympathy and love. These are the principles of heaven, and when they are revealed in the lives of human beings, we may know that Christ is formed within, the hope and glory. A congregation may be the poorest in the land, without music or outward show, but if it possesses these principles, the members can sing, for the joy of Christ is in their souls, and this they can offer as a sweet oblation to God." (Manuscript 123, 1899)

"When professing Christians reach the high standard which it is their privilege to reach, the simplicity of Christ will be maintained in all their worship. Forms and ceremonies and musical accomplishments are not the strength of the church. Yet these things have taken the place God should have, even as they did in the worship of the Jews." (*Evangelism* page 512)

"The Lord has revealed to me that when the heart is cleansed and sanctified, and the members of the church are partakers of the divine nature, a power will go forth from the church, who believe the truth, that will cause melody in the heart. Men and women will not then depend upon their instrumental music but on the power and grace of God, which will give fullness of joy. There is a work to be done in clearing away the rubbish which has been brought into the church. . . ." (*Evangelism* page 512)

**Principle #19: In many cases congregational singing will bring more of a blessing than the singing of a choir, regardless of how skilled the choir may be.**

"...Often the singing of simple hymns by the congregation has a charm that is not possessed by the singing of a choir, however skilled it may be." (*Evangelism* page 509)

"The singing is not always to be done by a few. As often as possible, let the entire congregation join." (*Testimonies* Volume 9 page 144)

**Principle #20:    Music should have beauty, pathos, and power.**

"...Music should have beauty, pathos, and power. Let the voices be lifted in songs of praise and devotion,  Call to your aid, if practicable, instrumental music, and let the glorious harmony ascend to God, an acceptable offering." (*Evangelism* page 505)

"There is something peculiarly sacred in the human voice. Its harmony and its subdued and heaven-inspired pathos exceeds every musical instrument. Vocal music is one of God's gifts to men, an instrument that cannot be surpassed or equaled when God's love abounds in the soul. Singing with the spirit and the understanding also is a great addition to devotional services in the house of God." (*Selected Messages* Volume 3 page 335)

**Principle #21:  Instrumental music, when lifted in glorious harmony, is an acceptable offering to God.**

"In the meetings held, let a number be chosen to take part in the song service. And let the singing be accompanied with music instruments skillfully handled. We are not to oppose the use of instrumental music in our work. This part of the service is to be carefully conducted; for the praise of God in song." (*Testimonies* Volume 9 page 144)

**Principle #22:  Religious worship, and everything connected with it, should be dignified, solemn and impressive.**

"Everything that is connected in any way with religious worship should be dignified, solemn, and impressive." (*Selected Messages* Volume 3 page 333)

"...Let us give no place to strange exercisings, which really take the mind away from the deep movings of the Holy Spirit. God's work is ever characterized by calmness and dignity..." (*Selected Messages* Volume 2 page 42)

"...Some are not satisfied with a meeting unless they have a powerful and happy time. They work for this and get up an excite-

ment of feeling. But the influence of such meetings is not benefi-
cial. When the happy flight of feeling is gone, they sink lower than
before the meeting because their happiness did not come from the
right source. The most profitable meetings for spiritual advancement
are those which are characterized with solemnity and deep searching of heart; each seeking to know himself and earnestly, and in deep
humility, seeking to learn of Christ." (*Testimonies* Volume 1 page
412)

"...A bedlam of noise shocks the senses and perverts that which
if conducted aright might be a blessing. The powers of satanic agencies blend with the din and noise to have a carnival, and this is termed
the Holy Spirit's working. . . . Those things which have been in the
past will be in the future. Satan will make music a snare by the way
in which it is conducted." (*Selected Messages* volume 2, page 36 and
37)

"The manner in which the meetings in Indiana have been carried
on, with noise and confusion, does not commend them to thoughtful,
intelligent minds. There is nothing in these demonstrations which will
convince the world that we have the truth. Mere noise and shouting are
no evidence of sanctification, or of the descent of the Holy Spirit. Your
wild demonstrations create only disgust in the minds of unbelievers.
The fewer of such demonstrations there are, the better it will be for the
actors and for the people in general. " (*Selected Messages* Volume 2
page 35)

"...Low songs, lewd gestures, expressions, and attitudes, deprave
the imagination and debase the morals. Every youth who habitually
attends such exhibitions will be corrupted in principle..." (*Messages
to Young People* page 380)

**Principle #23: The simplicity of Christ, rather than forms
and ceremonies, should characterize all our worship.**

"When professing Christians reach the high standard which it
is their privilege to reach, the simplicity of Christ will be maintained
in all their worship. Forms and ceremonies and musical accomplishments are not the strength of the church. Yet these things have taken
the place that God should have even as they did in the worship of the

Jews." (Manuscript 157, 1899)

"In their efforts to reach the people, the Lord's messengers are not to follow the ways of the world. In the meetings that are held, they are not to depend on worldly singers and theatrical display to awaken an interest. How can those who have no interest in the Word of God, who have never read His Word with a sincere desire to understand its truths, be expected to sing with the spirit and the understanding? How can their hearts be in harmony with the words of sacred song? How can the heavenly choir join in music that is only a form?" (*Testimonies* Volume 9 page 143)

**Principle #24: When the home is filled with singing that's soft, sweet and pure, there will be fewer words of censure and more of cheerfulness and joy.**

"...Let there be singing in the home, of songs that are sweet and pure, and there will be fewer words of censure and more of cheerfulness and hope and joy..." (*Education* page 168)

**Principle #25: God is not pleased with strange sounds and/or long drawn out notes that draw attention to the singer, for the music of heaven is beautiful, unselfish and harmonious.**

"In some churches I have heard solos that were altogether unsuitable for the service of the Lord's house. The long drawn out notes and peculiar sounds common in operatic singing are not pleasing to the angels. They delight to hear the simple songs of praise sung in a natural tone. The songs in which every word is uttered clearly, in a musical tone, are the songs that they join us in singing. They take up the refrain that is sung from the heart with the spirit and the understanding." (*Evangelism* page 510)

"Display is not religion nor sanctification. There is nothing more offensive in God's sight than a display of instrumental music when those taking part are not consecrated, are not making melody in their hearts to the Lord. The offering most sweet and acceptable in God's sight is a heart made humble by self-denial, by lifting the cross and following Jesus." (*Evangelism* page 510)

**Principle #26: God is not pleased when solos are filled with self.**

"Musical talent too often fosters pride and ambition for display, and singers have but little thought of the worship of God. Instead of leading minds to remembering God, it often causes them to forget Him." (Letter 6a, 1890, pages 11-12)

"Your singing is far from pleasing to the angel choir. Imagine yourself standing in the angel band elevating your shoulders, emphasizing the words, motioning your body and putting in the full volume of your voice. What kind of concert and harmony would there be with such an exhibition before the angels?" (*The Voice in Speech and Song* page 424)

Notice, there is nothing condemning current, or recently written music. Some beautiful songs have been written through the years, songs that are Christ-centered, and inspiring such as "There is a Saviour" and "To God be the Glory." There are many such songs, and the list will continue growing until the Lord comes. We do have a responsibility as followers of the Lamb, however, to test each song for its worth. To reject all contemporary music would be just as foolish as to accept all of it at face value. Sometimes it is not the song itself, but the way it is played, that becomes offensive to the Christian's ear. Rocked-up hymns could certainly have this effect, which is why we must consider all aspects of a song when proving what is acceptable to God.

As parents, teachers and a church, we have a solemn responsibility to teach our young people the paths of righteousness in music so that they won't be conformed to the standards of the world. God is not the author of confusion, and our music should reflect that fact by being simple, beautiful, serene, and calmly sung to the glory of God.

# 16

# The Great Controversy (Over Music!)

**Principle #27:** **Despite popular theories, your choice of music is a spiritual decision, having important ramifications both for this life and in eternity.**

W e've talked quite a bit about how the "great controversy" has been fought on the musical battleground. But while there is indeed a cosmic conflict being fought on a universal scale, God and the Devil are also involved in a struggle for the allegiance of every human heart.

God is waiting—anxiously waiting—for an invitation to come into your life and point you in the right spiritual direction. He wants to fill you with His Spirit and help you make right choices. And, since music is a spiritual choice, He wants to help you with that choice.

The nice thing about God's Word is that it speaks to so many areas of our life. In addition to the promise of salvation, God's Word also promises to give us the knowledge of His music when we choose Him. The right music is that important to God. He knows how powerful music can be. He knows that it can be used by anybody to drive home a message, and He wants to make sure that only the right messages are filling our hearts.

And so, in His efforts to re-establish His original purpose for music, God points out His music to us. Through the infinite power of His grace—the same grace that can give us salvation and bring us out of the old life—He is also seeking to direct us into His music.

Even if we've filled ourselves or exposed ourselves to music that's not God's, God's music can still touch and change us. And though God's music is designed to help us love and praise Him right now, we can also taste a little bit of heaven through the beauty of music. God wants us to have a living connection with Him, through meditation, prayer, and yes, music. Then, and only then, can He put that new song in our hearts.

If we spend our time looking into God's things, listening to the things of heaven, allowing Him to show us what His music is, if we spend our time attuned to His voice—then all the confusion, clamor, and noise of the earth won't be enough to confuse us. We will know God's sounds, the sounds of eternity, the sounds of music and praise, because we're tuned in to His voice.

And when we listen to the still, small voice of God, we will surely know His will. "Be still and know that I am God," we are told through the Psalmist. (Psalms 46:10) And it is when we are still and listening that we can hear God's voice above the noisy, clamoring music of this wicked world.

As long as we live on this earth, two strains of music will greet our ears. One is God's music, and it seems very strange to the sinner's ears. The other is the Devil's, a music that is very strange to the courts of God. And while the Devil has mixed-up may combinations of good and bad music, remember—it doesn't take much arsenic to spoil the stew.

There are two spirits working in this world, the Spirit of God which is light and life, and the spirit of Satan or darkness and death. Each of those spirits has a spiritual mission and purpose in the story of the great controversy. It stands to reason that the music that each spirit would use and control would have a spiritual purpose.

Music, then, is a spiritual matter—and choosing music is a spiritual choice. Don't be fooled: music is not neutral, harmless or just "a matter of taste." Some people don't understand this fact, for spiritual things are spiritually discerned. But choices in music are very spiritual decisions, and because of that fact, we all desperately need God's Spirit to help us make right the right choice. Otherwise, we really wouldn't know which direction to turn.

Although, in many ways, Satan has accomplished his personal vendetta to destroy man's image of God through music, God is still in control. People have praised God through music through ages past, and even today, God still has a people who praise Him through music untainted by Satan's counterfeit.

As I look around my world today, I don't think it's any different now than it was back then. The great disagreement between truth and evil, light and darkness, God and Satan, hasn't changed one iota. Each side still has a purpose and mission in the spiritual battle being fought all around us.

God's music is, and has always been, designed to praise Him: the Devil's music is, and has always been, designed to praise self, excitement, and human passions.

Yes, as it was in the days of Noah, Moses, Deborah, David, and so many other Bible characters, so it will be at the coming of the Son of Man. God has His music, and Satan has his. Music is no less powerful today than it was back in Bible times. It's powerful for good today; it was powerful for good back then. And this battle will continue until the day Jesus comes. Then the "Great Controversy" about music will be over. Then God's music will ring through the courts of heaven through the ceaseless ages of eternity. Amen and Amen.

# 17

# The "Style" of Worship in Heaven

There are many decisions to be made today about worship:

1. Should we have a pulpit or not?
2. What about overhead projectors?
3. How many songs should we sing?
4. What style of songs should we sing?
5. What should we hear from the pulpit?
6. Is there a proper mix of genders, races, and age groups represented in leadership?
5. Should we applaud or recognize the performer, and if so, how?

But while we are spending much time discussing how to worship, there seems to be little concern for the real purpose of worship, or what the God of heaven wants us to do when we worship Him. We are a "me first" society; it's what makes me happy that is considered appropriate.

The angels are the best resource to study as to what pleases God in music. They praise God continually and glorify Him through song. Much is written about angels and our relationship with them in praising the Father, and I have found it exciting to learn how we can be involved with them in praising God even now. We may also learn lessons from the angels, lessons that will guide us in the direction of truth and help to reveal the counterfeit.

It's incredible to think that every time we come together to worship, angels are listening to our testimonies, songs, and prayers. Not only are they listening, but they are supplementing our praise with the angelic host above.

Some key points I've learned through the study of angel music include:

1. God created music for praise and worship.
2. God has given us a New Song of deliverance.
3. The angels praise God continually.
4. We can learn the songs of the angels and heaven right here on earth.
5. Music brings vivid impressions to one's heart. It can be warm, pure, loving, spiritual thoughts, or it can produce evil, violent, disrespectful, uncontrolled passions that destroy the soul.
6. If we praise God with spirit and understanding in our songs, the heavenly musicians will take up the strain and join in the song of thanksgiving.

This brings us to an important question: what does it mean to sing with spirit and understanding? Is singing in the church just something to get Sabbath school started? Do we use it to get the congregation quiet and ready to start the meeting?

Many times, when the song service is over, I have heard the leader say, "now let's turn to our opening song…"

We seem to have a habit of thinking that music is getting the people ready for the meeting to come, when in reality the service begins when we sing the first song. If the church needs to come to attention and become reverent, why not start by having prayer. If you mention prayer, the congregation will understand that it is time to be quiet and start our worship.

All too often we give no thought to the songs we sing. It's easy to make no preparation, or just say "let us sing number whatever." I have heard songs services that either start in the front of the hymnal, and progressively go a few pages ahead, or start at the back of the hymnal and work to the front. We are missing out on a real blessing when we do this, for the hymnal is topically arranged and one can develop a real message by singing songs on a certain subject such as forgiveness, the second coming of Christ, the Sabbath, the state of the dead, and the list goes on.

If song leaders want to use several subjects in a song service, they can do so by tying thoughts together. For example, songs on acceptance of Jesus could be sung as preparation for songs on the second coming. As you tie these hymns together, your narrative between songs can be very important to the message you are trying to present.

When we point out the message in a hymn, we help the congregation to sing with spirit and understanding. A good example of this would be Hymn 412 in the *SDA Church Hymnal*, written by F. E. Belden, "Covered with His life."

This is a hymn about forgiveness of sin, a hymn about righteousness by faith. This hymn helps us to realize our sinful condition, and how we can be covered with His life, and accept His robe of righteousness. Notice how in the last verse the author was able to bring in the story of salvation in just four lines:

> *Reconciled by His death for my sin,*
> *Justified by His life pure and clean,*
> *Sanctified by obeying His word,*
> *Glorified when returneth my Lord.*

If we understand what the hymn is saying to us we will no longer sing it by rote. It is not just another hymn, for it has become a part of us. The spiritual ear alone, one whose ears are listening to God through the reading of His Word and searching for truth by the Holy Spirit, can hear the harmony of heavenly voices who join them in ascribing praise to God and His Son. I have experienced this many times in congregational singing, and in choirs I have been a part of. What a joy it is to learn the song of the angels now so that we may be better prepared to sing it when we join their shining ranks!

"As our Redeemer leads us to the threshold of the Infinite, flushed with the glory of God, we may catch the themes of praise and thanksgiving from the heavenly choir round about the throne; and as the echo of the angels' song is awakened in our earthly homes, hearts will be drawn closer to the heavenly singers. Heaven's communion begins on earth. We learn here the keynote of its praise." (*Education* page 168)

## *Notable Quotes:*

"Let us all bear in mind that in every assembly of the saints below are angels of God, listening to the testimonies, songs, and prayers. Let us remember that our praises are supplemented by the choirs of the angelic host above ... Let the love of God be the burden of the speaker's utterance. Let it be expressed in simple language in every song of praise..." (*Testimonies* Volume 6 page 367)

"...When human beings sing with the spirit and understanding, heavenly musicians take up the strain and join in the song of thanksgiving..." (*Testimonies* Volume 9 page 143)

"...The spiritual ear alone can hear the harmony of heavenly voices ... And as the Lord's army of workers here below sing their songs of praise, the choir above joins with them in ascribing praise to God and His Son." (*Acts of the Apostles* page 153, 154)

"...All the inhabitants of heaven unite in praising God. Let us learn the song of the angels now, that we may sing it when we join their shining ranks..." (*Patriarchs and Prophets* page 289)

"The melody of praise is the atmosphere of heaven, and when heaven comes in touch with the earth there is music and song, thanksgiving, and the voice of melody." (*Messages to Young People* page 291)

"I have heard the angels sing. They do not sing as you are singing tonight. They sing with reverence, with meaning. Their hearts are in their expressions of songs. Now let us try again and see if we can put our hearts into singing this song." (Ellen G. White Volume 3 page 384)

"...But If the saints fixed their eyes upon the prize before them and glorified God by praising Him, the angels would bear the glad tidings to the city, and the angels in the city would touch their golden harps and sing with a loud voice, Alleluia and the heavenly arches would ring with their lovely songs." (*Early Writings* page 39)

# 18

# When the Sacred Gets Mixed with the Common

One of the members of the online SDA community in which I take part, Ben Tupper, recently mentioned that the greatest need in the Adventist church is the recovery of a sense of holiness in worship. In our quest for numbers, acceptability, and comfort, it seems that a biblical sense of holiness has largely been displaced by a rather crude "folksiness."

In studying this issue, I looked up the four different words used for reverence in *Strong's Concordance*. Interestingly enough, they all had a common thread— awe, fear, holiness, and respect.

This is the type of attitude God asks us to bring when we come to worship Him.

"Ye shall keep My Sabbaths, and reverence My sanctuary; I am the Lord." (Leviticus 19:30)

"And He said, Draw not nigh hither: put off thy shoes from off thy feet, for the place whereon thou standest is holy ground." (Exodus 3:5)

"...The Lord is in His holy temple: let all the earth keep silent before Him." (Habukkuk 2:20)

"...for mine house shall be called an house of prayer for all people." (Isaiah 56:7)

"Keep thy foot when thou goest to the house of God, and be more ready to hear, than to give the sacrifice of fools: for they consider not that they do evil." (Ecclesiastes 5:1)

"But as for me, I will come into Thy house in the multitude of Thy mercy: and in Thy fear will I worship toward Thy holy temple." (Psalms 5:7)

"Wherefore we receiving a kingdom which cannot be moved,

let us have grace, whereby we may serve God acceptably with reverence and godly fear: for our God is a consuming fire." (Hebrews 12:28-29)

"God is greatly to be feared in the assembly of the saints, and to be had in reverence of all them that are about Him." (Psalms 89:7)

In the words of a time-honored hymn:

*With reverence let the saints appear,*
*And bow before the Lord;*
*His high commands with reverence hear,*
*And tremble at His word.*

*O Jesus, Lord of earth and heaven,*
*Our life and joy, to Thee*
*Be honor, thanks, and blessing given*
*Through all eternity.*

by Isaac Watts

### Notable Quotes:

"If some have to wait a few minutes before the meeting begins, let them maintain a true spirit of devotion by silent meditation, keeping the heart uplifted to God in prayer that the service may be of special benefit to their own hearts and lead to the conviction and conversion of other souls. They should remember that heavenly messengers are in the house. We all lose much sweet communion with God by our restlessness, by not encouraging moments of reflection and prayer. The spiritual condition needs to be often reviewed and the mind and heart drawn toward the Sun of Righteousness. If when the people come into the house of worship, they have genuine reverence for the Lord and bear in mind that they are in His presence, there will be a sweet eloquence in silence. The whispering and laughing and talking which might be without sin in a common business place should find no sanction in the house where God is worshiped. The mind should be prepared to hear the word of God, that it may have due weight and suitably impress the heart." (*Testimonies* Volume 5 page 492)

"When the benediction is pronounced, all should still be quiet, as if fearful of losing the peace of Christ. Let all pass out without jostling or loud talking, feeling that they are in the presence of God, that His eye is resting upon them, and that they must act as in His visible presence. Let there be no stopping in the aisles to visit or gossip, thus blocking them up so that others cannot pass out. The precincts of the church should be invested with a sacred reverence. It should not be made a place to meet old friends and visit and introduce common thoughts and worldly business transactions. These should be left outside the church. God and angels have been dishonored by the careless, noisy laughing and shuffling of feet heard in some places." (*Testimonies* Volume 5 page 493-494)

"It is too true that reverence for the house of God has become almost extinct. Sacred things and places are not discerned; the holy and exalted are not appreciated. Is there not a cause for the want of fervent piety in our families? Is it not because the high standard of religion is left to trail in the dust? God gave rules of order, perfect and exact, to His ancient people. Has His character changed? Is He not the great and mighty God who rules in the heaven of heavens? Would it not be well for us often to read the directions given by God Himself to the Hebrews, that we who have the light of the glorious truth shining upon us may imitate their reverence for the house of God? We have abundant reason...even to be more thoughtful and reverential in our worship than had the Jews. But an enemy has been at work to destroy our faith in the sacredness of Christian worship." (*Testimonies* Volume 5 page 495-496)

"God has children, many of them, in the Protestant churches, and a large number in the Catholic churches, who are more true to obey the light and to the very best of their knowledge than a large number among Sabbath keeping Adventists who do not walk in the light..." (*Selected Messages* Volume 3 page 386)

"...Young persons assemble to sing, and, although professed Christians, frequently dishonor God and their faith by their frivolous conversation and their choice of music. Sacred music is not congenial to their taste..." (*Testimonies* Volume 1 page 506)

"If you truly belong to Christ, you will have opportunities for witnessing for Him. You will be invited to attend places of amusement, and then it will be that you will have an opportunity to testify to your Lord. If you are true to Christ then, you will not try to form excuses for your non-attendance, but will plainly and modestly declare that you are a child of God, and your principles would not allow you to be in a place, even for one occasion, where you could not invite the presence of your Lord." (*Messages to Young People* page 370)

"From the sacredness which was attached to the earthly sanctuary, Christians may learn how they should regard the place where the Lord meets with His people. There has been a great change, not for the better, but for the worse, in the habits and customs of the people in reference to religious worship. The precious, the sacred, things which connect us with God are fast losing their hold upon our minds and hearts, and are being brought down to the level of common things. The reverence which the people had anciently for the sanctuary where they met with God in sacred service has largely passed away. Nevertheless, God Himself gave the order of His service, exalting it high above everything of a temporal nature." (*Testimonies* Volume 5 page 491)

"In the minds of many there are no more sacred thoughts connected with the house of God than the most common place. Some will enter the place of worship with their hats on, in soiled, dirty clothes, such do not realize that they are to meet with God and holy angels. There should be a radical change in this matter all through our churches. Ministers themselves need to elevate their ideals, to have finer susceptibilities in regard to it. It is a feature of the work that has been sadly neglected. Because of the irreverence in attitude, dress and deportment, and lack of a worshipful frame of mind, God has often turned His face away from those assembled for His worship." (*Testimonies* Volume 5 page 498-499)

"When a church has been raised up and left uninstructed on

these points, the minister has neglected his duty and will have to give an account to God for the impressions he allowed to prevail. Unless correct ideas of true worship and true reverence are impressed upon the people, there will be a growing tendency to place the sacred and eternal on a level with common things, and those professing the truth will be an offense to God and a disgrace to religion. They can never with their uncultivated ideas, appreciate a pure and holy heaven, and be prepared to join with the worshipers in the heavenly courts above, where all is purity and perfection, where every being has perfect reverence for God and His holiness." (*Testimonies* Volume 5 page 500)

# Appendix A

# Warnings Against the Theatrical

I have included all of these statements because, as I reminisce about my years in youth evangelism, I recall some very talented young people who had a flare for theater. One I think of is a young lady with unusual talent in art and drama. It was thirty years ago when she worked with our team. Today, she is working for Disney as an artist. I think of others who have left the faith who were very talented in writing and acting. I allowed drama in our witness teams, and now after all these years I can see where God's counsel is right, and I am sorry for not heeding it back then. I give this testimony to our youth leaders, hoping that they can avoid the same mistake. There are many churches and schools today that encourage drama, but God still gives us the straight testimony. May God bless all who have the heavy responsibility of leading God's youth into paths of righteousness.

"It is not safe for the Lord's workers to take part in worldly entertainments. Association with worldliness in musical lines is looked upon as harmless by some Sabbath keepers. But such ones are on dangerous ground. Thus Satan seeks to lead men and women astray, and thus he has gained control of souls. So smooth, so plausible is the working of the enemy that his wiles are not expected, and many church members become lovers of pleasure more than lovers of God." (*Selected Messages* Volume 3 page 332)

"Among the most dangerous resorts for pleasure is the theater. Instead of being a school of morality and virtue, as is so often claimed, it is the very hotbed of immorality. Vicious habits and sinful propensities are strengthened and confirmed by these entertainments. Low songs, lewd gestures, expressions, and attitudes, deprave the imagination and debase the morals. Every youth who habitually attends such exhibitions will be corrupted in principle. There is no influence in our land more powerful to poison the imagination, to destroy religious impressions, and to blunt the relish for the tranquil pleasures and sober realities of life than theatrical amusements..." (*Counsels to Parents, Teachers and Students* page 334)

"He (Satan) does not wish people to have a knowledge of their Maker, and he is well pleased if he can set in operation games and theatrical performances that will so confuse the senses of the youth that the God of heaven will be forgotten..." (*Messages to Young People* page 214)

"The true Christian will not desire to enter any place of amusement or engage in any diversion upon which he cannot ask the blessing of God. He will not be found in the theater..." (*Messages to Young People* page 398)

"I have a message for those in charge of our work. Do not encourage the men who are to engage in this work to think that they must proclaim the solemn, sacred message in a theatrical style. Not one jot or tittle of anything theatrical is to be brought into our work. God's cause is to have a sacred, heavenly mold. Let everything connected with giving the message for this time bear the divine impress. Let nothing of a theatrical nature be permitted, for this would spoil the sacredness of the work...In my very first labors the message was given that all theatrical performances in connection with the preaching of present truth were to be discouraged and forbidden..." (*Evangelism* page 137)

"...It is not for the workers to seek for methods by which they can make a show, consuming time in theatrical performances and musical display, for this benefits no one..." (*Fundamentals of Christian Education* page 253)

"...The work in the large cities is to be done after Christ's order, not after the order of a theatrical performance. It is not a theatrical performance that glorifies God, but the presentation of the truth in the love of Christ." (*Testimonies* Volume 9 page 142)

"Another element invading modern Christian worship is drama. I have no moral problem with using some visual aids to help people better understand Bible truth. God asked prophets like Ezekiel and Jeremiah to do this (Jeremiah 32:14 and Ezekiel 5:1-4). But some argue that this justifies the dramatic stage productions with raucous applause that are making their way into our churches. The problem is that many professed Christians have become so over stimulated from a steady diet of movies, TV, and videos that a simple, reverent worship service without drama, drums, and dancing deacons seems boring by comparison. Many now come to church to be entertained rather than to give their worship, praise, songs, and offerings." Amazing Facts Newsletter, "Theatrical Theology"

"We might see a different order of things should a number consecrate themselves wholly to God, and then devote their talents to the Sabbath School work, ever advancing in knowledge, and educating themselves so that they would be able to instruct others as to the best methods to employ in the work; but it is not for the workers to seek for methods by which they can make a show, consuming time in theatrical performances and musical display, for this benefits no one. It does no good to train the children to make speeches for special occasions. They should be won to Christ, and instead of expending time, money, and effort to make a display, let the whole effort be made to gather sheaves for the harvest." (*Counsels on Sabbath School Work* page 153)

"Those who do the work of the Lord in the cities must put forth calm, steady, devoted effort for the education of the people. While they are to labor earnestly to interest the hearers, and to hold this interest, yet at the same time they must carefully guard against anything that borders on sensationalism. In this age of extravagance and outward show, when men think it necessary to make a display in order to gain success, God's chosen messengers are to show the fallacy of spending means needlessly for effect. As they labor with simplicity, humility, and graceful dignity, avoiding everything of a theatrical nature, their work will make a lasting impression for good." (*Gospel Workers* page 346)

"God is not pleased by your large outlay of means to advertise your meetings, and by the display made in other features of your work. The display is out of harmony with the principles of the Word of God. He is dishonored by your expensive preparations. At times you do that which is represented to me as the shredding of wild gourds into the pot. This display makes the truth taste too strongly of the dish. Man is exalted. The truth is not advanced, but hindered. Sensible men and women can see that the theatrical performances are not in harmony with the solemn message that you bear." (*Evangelism* page 127)

"Our success will depend on carrying forward the work in the simplicity in which Christ carried it forward, without any theatrical display." (*Evangelism* page 139)

"Ministers are not to preach men's opinions, not to relate anecdotes, get up theatrical performances, not to exhibit self; but as though they were in the presence of God and of the Lord Jesus Christ, they are to preach the Word. Let them not bring levity into the work of the ministry, but let them preach the Word in a manner that will leave a most solemn impression upon those who hear." (*Evangelism* page 207)

"In our work we are not to go onto a hilltop to shine. We are not told that we must make a special, wonderful display. The truth must be proclaimed in the highways and the byways, and thus work is to be done by sensible, rational methods. The life of every worker, if he is under the training of the Lord Jesus Christ, will reveal the excellence of His life. The work that Christ did in our world is to be our example, as far as display is concerned. We are to keep as far from the theatrical and the extraordinary as Christ kept in His work. Sensation is not religion, although religion will exert its own pure, sacred, uplifting, sanctifying influence, bringing spiritual life, and salvation." (*Evangelism* page 396)

"In their efforts to reach the people, the Lord's messengers are not to follow the ways of the world. In the meetings that are held, they are not to depend on worldly singers and theatrical display to awaken an interest. How can those who have no interest in the Word of God, who have never read His Word with a sincere desire to understand its truths, be expected to sing with the spirit and the understanding? How can their hearts be in harmony with the words of sacred song? How can the heavenly choir join in music that is only a form?" (*Evangelism* page 508)

"I see that great reformation must take place in the ministry before it shall be what God would have it. Ministers in the desk have no license to behave like theatrical performers, assuming attitudes and expressions calculated for effect. They do not occupy the sacred desk as actors, but as teachers of solemn truths. There are also fanatical ministers, who, in attempting to preach Christ, pound the desk before them, as if this bodily exercise profited anything. Such antics lend no force to the truths uttered, but, on the contrary, disgust men and women of calm judgment and elevated views. It is the duty of men who give themselves to the ministry to leave all coarseness and boisterous conduct outside the desk at least." (*Evangelism* page 640)

"All the sang-froid, which is so common, the theatrical gestures, all lightness and trifling, all jesting and joking, must be seen by the one who wears Christ's yoke to be "not convenient"—an offense to God and a denial of Christ. It unfits the mind for solid thought and solid labor. It makes men inefficient, superficial, and spiritually diseased. . . ." (*Evangelism* page 644)

"The minister of Christ should be a man of prayer, a man of piety; cheerful, but never coarse and rough, jesting or frivolous. A spirit of frivolity may be in keeping with the profession of clowns and theatrical performers, but it is altogether beneath the dignity of a man who is chosen to stand between the living and the dead, and to be a mouthpiece for God." (*Gospel Workers* page 132)

"Let there be no oddities or eccentricities of movement on the part of those who speak the Word of truth, for such things will weaken the impression that should be made by the Word. We must be guarded, for Satan is determined, if possible, to intermingle with religious services his evil influence. Let there be no theatrical display, for this will not help to strengthen belief in the Word of God. Rather, it will divert attention to the human instrument." (Letter 352, 1908)

"In the discourses, let nothing of a theatrical nature be introduced, no sharp thrusts given. We cannot expect that eyes that have been blind will be at once opened to see all things clearly. Let labor be put forth wisely for those who are interested. Show those who have seen the truth, how to experience its power in their hearts. Thus the truth imparted will be as a nail driven in a sure place. Many are ignorant of vital godliness—of truth in the life-practice. On the part of these uninstructed ones, there must be a practical reception of Bible truth. The Lord will work with power upon the hearts of all who seek him and who prayerfully study his Word." (Advent Review and Sabbath Herald, DT 02-14-07)

"David's dancing in reverent joy before God has been cited by pleasure lovers in justification of the fashionable modern dance, but there is no ground for such an argument. In our day dancing is associated with folly and midnight reveling. Health and morals are sacrificed to pleasure. By the frequenters of the ballroom, God is not an object of thought and reverence; prayer or the song of praise would be felt to be out of place in their assemblies. This test should be decisive. Amusements that have a tendency to weaken the love for sacred things and lessen our joy in the service of God are not to be sought by Christians..." (*Patriarchs and Prophets* page 707)

# Appendix B

# Spirit of Prophecy Quotes on False Revivals

Ellen White wrote a chapter in *The Great Controversy* called "Modern Revivals," discussing the final religious movements that would take place in our world before the Lord would come.

"...Before the final visitation of God's judgments upon the earth, there will be among the people of the Lord such a revival of primitive godliness as has not been witnessed since apostolic times.... The enemy of souls desires to hinder this work. And before the time for such a movement shall come, he will endeavor to prevent it by introducing a counterfeit. In those churches which he can bring under his deceptive power, he will make it appear that God's special blessing is poured out, there will be manifest what is thought to be a great religious interest. Multitudes will exult that God is working marvelously for them when the work is that of another spirit under religious guise, Satan will seek to extend his influence over the Christian world." (*Great Controversy* page 464)

"Popular revivals are too often carried by appeals to the imagination, by exciting the emotions, by gratifying the love for what is new and startling. Converts thus gained have little desire to listen to Bible truth, little interest in the testimony of prophets and apostles. Unless a religious service has something of a sensational character, it has no attractions for them..." (*Great Controversy* page 463)

"...Picnics, church theatricals, church fairs, personal display, fine houses, have banished thoughts of God..." (*Great Controversy* page 463)

"...Were Jesus to enter the churches of today and behold the feasting and unholy traffic there conducted in the name of religion, would He not drive out those desecrators, as He banished the money-changers from the temple?" (*Great Controversy* page 474)

"One of the most powerful elements of worship that has become extremely divisive is music. From the ancient Roman orgies and primitive tribal war dances, to the insane behavior at modern concerts and sporting events, pagan music with its heavy, syncopated rhythms has been used to excite carnal passions and wild behavior. Many Christian churches have now embraced this same music. And it's not just the loud "Christian rock." I have seen whole congregations that look like they have been mesmerized through the New Age music with shallow, repetitive lyrics sung over and over. If Jesus tells us not to pray in vain repetition, then it is likely He does not want us singing that way either." (see Matthew 6:7) Doug Batchelor, Amazing Facts

"Blessed is the man that walketh not in the counsel of the ungodly. But his delight is in the law of the Lord; and in His law doth he meditate day and night. And he shall be like a tree planted by the rivers of water, that bringeth forth his fruit in his season; his leaf also shall not wither; and whatsoever he doeth shall prosper." (Psalms 1:1-3)

"It is only as the law of God is restored to its rightful position that there can be a revival of primitive faith and godliness among His professed people. "Thus saith the Lord, Stand ye in the ways, and see, and ask for the old paths, where is the good way, and walk therein, and ye shall find rest for your souls."" (*The Faith I Live* By page 326, Jeremiah 6:16)

# Appendix C

# 27 Practical Principles for Choosing Heavenly Music

### Principle #1
"Not I, but Christ, be honored, loved, exalted..."

### Principle #2
Satan has a counterfeit for every one of God's gifts, and that includes even Christian music.

### Principle #3
When the beat overshadows the words, or the physical side of music takes precedence over the intellectual, the music is from beneath.

### Principle #4
We can trust God's Word to settle the music question for us.

### Principle #5
Just as a little poison spoils the stew, so a little error spoils the song.

### Principle #6
As children of God, we need to be listening to His music as we grow into His image

### Principle #7
God is looking for Christians who will stand "on the Plain of Dura," refusing to succumb to Satan's temptations, bow down to his image, or listen to his music.

### *Principle #8*
The music of Christ will not be the same as the world's.

### *Principle #9*
If we come to Jesus and surrender to Him just as we are, He will change our tastes in music.

### *Principle #10*
Our job is to judge music, not people.

### *Principle #11*
We are not to give up on God's children, for many who seem to have little or no spiritual potential will be truly converted and become ardent workers in God's cause.

### *Principle #12*
While music is one of the greatest blessings given by God, it is also one of Satan's primary tools to ensnare the young.

### *Principle #13*
Music can be a powerful witnessing tool in the hands of dedicated Christian youth.

### *Principle #14*
God's music can be very effective in helping us to encourage others, resist temptation, and memorize Scripture.

### *Principle #15*
Even simple songs, when sung to the glory of God, may touch the hearts of others and win them to Christ.

### *Principle #16*
It is not loud singing that is needed, but soft, silvery tones. We should train our voices to sing in this heavenly manner.

### *Principle #17*
God wants us to sing with the spirit and understanding, and when we do, the angels will join our song.

### *Principle #18*

The nearer Christ's people come to correct, harmonious singing, the more God is glorified, the church is blessed, and unbelievers will be favorably impressed.

### *Principle #19*

In many cases congregational singing will bring more of a blessing than the singing of a choir, regardless of how skilled the choir may be.

### *Principle #20*

Music should have beauty, pathos, and power.

### *Principle #21*

Instrumental music, when lifted in glorious harmony, is an acceptable offering to God.

### *Principle #22*

Religious worship, and everything connected with it, should be dignified, solemn, and impressive.

### *Principle #23*

The simplicity of Christ, rather than forms and ceremonies, should characterize all our worship.

### *Principle #24*

When the home is filled with singing that's soft, sweet and pure, there will be fewer words of censure and more of cheerfulness and joy.

### *Principle #25*

God is not pleased with strange sounds and/or long drawn out notes that draw attention to the singer, for the music of heaven is beautiful, unselfish and harmonious.

### *Principle #26*

God is not pleased when solos are filled with self.

### *Principle #27*
Despite popular theories, your choice of music is a spiritual decision, having important ramifications both for this life and in eternity.

# Special Stories

*Favorite Stories from my days at the Voice of Prophecy, in youth evangelism and with H.M.S. Richards, Sr. (among others).*

### Story #1:
### *"Li'l Liz' I Love Ya"*

One of the greatest experiences of my youth was singing first tenor for the Atlantic Union College quartet. I was only in academy when they asked me, and I think I was their last hope, but what a thrill it was for me!

That year the Ted Mack Talent Show came to Worchester, Massachusetts. This was about thirty miles from Atlantic Union College, and local newspapers ran ads inviting talent to audition for the show. Our quartet talked about it, and, just for the fun of it, decided to give it a try.

Our palms were pretty sweaty on the day of the audition! The hall was full of talent, fine musicians competing in categories ranging from serious music to comedy—the one we had chosen. One by one the contestants were asked to perform. When our turn came, we sang "Li'l Liz' I Love Ya," a fun little song that was popular with quartets of the day. The words went like this:

*I had a dream the other night, I dreamt I was in love,*
*I dreamt I saw a maiden fair, beside the garden wall,*
*Honey, honey, honey, honey,*

*Chorus*

*Li'l Liz' I love ya, honey, oh how I love ya, honey,*
*Love ya in the springtime in the fall, Li'l Liz' I love ya honey,*
*Oh how I love ya honey, love you best of all.*

We had added several funny little verses of our own, and the one I liked best went like this:

*Now my gal lives in a big brick house,*
*And my gal lives the same.*
*And my gal lives in the county jail,*
*But, it's a brick house just the same.*

This drew snickers from the audience, of course, and we had a lot of fun doing it.

"If you're going to be on the program, we'll let you know," the talent show manager said as we walked out the door. We didn't know what it would mean to get involved, but we had a good time anyway.

Within a few days word came that we'd passed the audition. We were very happy about that, and practiced many hours to learn the song the best we could. On the night of the big performance about five carloads of students and the Dean of Men from AUC went with us. And, would you believe it, we won first place! Wow! What excitement filled our hearts!

The dean led the way home and the five cars circled the campus, tooting their horns. The next step was to go to the next level of competition, and the finals would be onstage in New York City itself. We were elated about the opportunity. The cash prize would be a big help for college expenses, and the lure of the big city and stage was a very exciting thing for my tenth grade mind. My friends were excited, too, and that made me feel even better. I was starting to think I might be onstage in the musical spotlight someday, when the bottom dropped out of my dream.

"I'm sorry, but you can't go on in the competition," the college president informed the three college men in our group. Evidently the Ted Mack Competition was sponsored by Old Gold Cigarettes, a piece of information the college had recently learned.

"You can't represent our school in a program sponsored by big tobacco," he said in effect. And with that, our competitive career skidded to an unceremonious halt. I was very disappointed, to say the least. I didn't understand what was going on.

"Maybe they'll change their mind and let us go," I told my friends. In my youthful exuberance, I had failed to see the big picture. I knew there was a war going on in this world, a war between Christ and Satan. I knew Satan concocted counterfeits for each of God's blessings, such as false doctrines, a false Sabbath, false principles for family living and false ways of worship. But it didn't occur to me then that Satan might be backstage in New York, managing everything from the spotlights to the music to the spirit of showmanship.

I now know that God was in AUC's decision, and the college did

115

the right thing. But it would have been hard for me to imagine, at that low moment in my life, that someday I'd thank those men for keeping, or at least trying to keep, my priorities straight.

As the next school year rolled around, I started to make some bad decisions in my life. I was a junior in high school, in the process of growing up, when I found myself climbing fool's hill. My rebellion was not severe: I never turned my back on the church. But I did do things I had learned were wrong, like going to movies, playing ball on Sabbath, and trading in some of my more conservative friends for those with more "liberal" minds.

During this time in my life, I became a real trial to my parents. I wasn't interested in school anymore; I wanted to experiment with life. I was making bad choices, using spare time unwisely, thinking how nice it would be to taste the world and all its allurements.

The whole Ted Mack episode really upset me, too. I'd been offered a chance to have fun, then lost out on the opportunity. I tried to hide much of my feelings and doings from my parents, but as it turned out, they knew a lot more than I thought.

My junior year ended, and I looked forward to sharing my senior year with friends at South Lancaster Academy. I would be free, free at last to taste the world and all it had to offer. But my mother, decisive Yankee that she was, had seen quite enough of my leanings. She had plans for me of her own, and with a little help from my brother, she managed to "send me packing." She wanted me to have new friends, a new start, and the solid Christian influence of my brother Wayne and his lovely wife, Virginia. Which is how I found myself spending my senior year in academy, as well as my college days, not in the hallowed halls of AUC, but at Southern Missionary College.

## Story #2:
### *When the Crowd Didn't Clap*

One experience I will never forget happened while I was singing with the Adelphian Quartet at Southern Missionary College. We
were singing with Marilyn Dillow, who was later to sing for *It is Written* under her married name, Marilyn Cotton. Marilyn sang with the
quartet on occasion, and at this particular time we were on our way to
a youth congress in Asheville, North Carolina.

It was Friday afternoon, and, having the radio on, we happened
to hear an advertisement for an all-night gospel sing at Asheville's
civic auditorium. Since our music centered mostly around hymns, we
had never experienced a gospel sing before.

"I wonder if we could find some new music by attending?" one
of our group suggested. After some conversation, we decided to stop
and check things out.

Except for Wayne, we were college kids with no money. Our
plan was to arrive at the gospel sing in our uniforms, and hope that the
ticket office would recognize us as a quartet and let us in free.

Our plan seemed to be working, for the first lady who saw us
showed us right to the stage door. She thought we were on the program, but Wayne explained our situation to a man backstage who was
checking in the singers.

"We just want to listen for music ideas," Wayne told the man.

"You never know," the man said. "If things start getting dull
later in the program, we might have a time when you can sing." He
motioned for someone to come and audition us, and, before we knew
what was happening, we were taken to a room with a piano.

"Come and play," the man motioned to Marilyn, supposing she
was our pianist.

"We don't use the piano," Wayne explained. "We sing acap-
pella."

"Oh!" the man replied, and seemed very surprised, but asked us
to sing for him anyway. Jack blew the pitch pipe and we sang "The
Old Rugged Cross." It was an uncomplicated arrangement—no frills,
just the plain message in simple style. The man's face was expression-
less, so we couldn't tell what he was thinking. But he asked us to sing

another song, and we sang "The City of Light," a song composed by a student at Oakwood College.

"Go backstage and wait," he told us when we finished the song. "We might use you later in the program."

We felt a little nervous standing around with all the famous gospel quartets and trios that were advertised features for the evening, but we did as we were told and soon the program started. The first quartet introduced was one many would recognize, for they were one of the most popular gospel quartets in the '50s.

The place went wild with whistles and thunderous applause when they appeared up front. Then they sang for about twelve minutes, and came backstage. The audience wanted more, of course, so after another round of thunderous applause, the quartet went onstage again. Right at that moment our quartet wasn't really sure which spirit was in charge—one of praising God or praise and adoration of men. The prevailing spirit soon became evident in the next song, which was entitled "Hallelujah Boogie." That's when we knew we were in the wrong place!

The quartet and Marilyn huddled together, discussing whether to make a quick exit or stay a bit longer. We decided to stay, in hopes that the music might somehow improve. Before we knew it, the first quartet came offstage and the emcee went out to introduce the next group of singers. Much to our surprise, he started talking about this college quartet from Chattanooga.

"They've just happened in," he told the audience, "and they sing acapella."

We were stunned to be second on the program, but the audience gave a polite applause as we walked on stage. Wayne went to the microphone, introduced us and said we would sing *The Old Rugged Cross*.

When we finished there was very little applause. Then we really thought we were in the wrong place. Not that we were used to people clapping for us—we just didn't know what to think.

We sang a second song, *Have You Been in The Garden With Jesus, alone with the Savior in prayer*, and this time there was no applause.

"Let's sing one more song and leave," Wayne whispered to us. That's when he chose *The Song of Heaven and Homeland*, that hymn about angel music that meant so much to me.

*"Sometimes I hear strange music like none 'ere heard before,"* we sang, *"come floating softly earthward as thro' heav'n's open door; It seems like angel voices, in strains of joy and love, that swell the mighty chorus, around the throne above."*

All this time the audience was so quiet you could hear a pin drop. Meanwhile Marilyn, who was off stage behind a curtain, added a beautiful obligato to the harmony of the song. When she sang that part, it was truly like you could hear an angel's voice singing off in the distance. The whole song was so simple yet beautiful, it really made you think you were right under the portals of heaven, listening to angel music as it wafted down through the gates.

There was silence when we finished the song, so we nodded at the audience and hurried offstage. The emcee was just starting to introduce the next group when the audience started to lightly applaud. They kept it up, 'til the emcee asked if they wanted to hear more of *that* kind of music. Then they kept on applauding 'til he called us back.

We sang for another twenty minutes without one round of applause. Until the end, that is, when they let us know they really did appreciate our songs.

"Don't ever change your music," one of the singers waiting to perform in a trio said as we came offstage. "Your music is of God. I know some of our music doesn't please Him."

I've been involved in many musical experiences over the years, but this has been one that I've cherished. Why didn't the audience clap? It wasn't because they didn't appreciate the music, for they let us know they did. I think there was something sacred, something holy, going on that night in the civic auditorium.

It wasn't due to any talent we had, for there was plenty of talent backstage. Myself, I think it was the power of simple and sacred music, accompanied by the working of God's Holy Spirit, quieting an otherwise boisterous crowd. It was as close as we could come to the music of heaven, being played out on the theatre of this world. God honored our music by speaking, ever so quietly, to the hearts of all who would listen.

### Story #3:
### Ruby

One summer while working as a singing evangelist in Morganton, North Carolina, I met an unforgettable lady by the name of Ruby. I was working with Elder Archer Livengood at the time, and after taking me with him on quite a few visits, he sent me out on my own.

That was when I met Ruby. She was in her early thirties at the time, and a very heavy smoker. Ruby seemed to smoke one cigarette right after another, and read racy romance novels just as voraciously. Yet God was working on her heart, for she felt drawn to our meetings.

"I've never heard anything like this before," she told me. "Elder Livengood really knows his Bible, and I feel God sent me to these meetings because I need help."

When she told me her story, I began to see that she really did need the help of our Heavenly Father in her life. She had left her husband in another state, and was in the middle of filing for divorce. Just months before, Ruby had been eight months pregnant. Unfortunately, her husband came home from work one night and started beating her. He became more and more violent, and finished up the evening by throwing her on the floor. There he repeatedly jumped on her, killing the baby and leaving her for dead.

"God spared my life," Ruby told me. "Now I feel I have a reason to live." The Holy Spirit was working on her heart, and she really wanted to respond.

"How do I become baptized?" she wanted to know. What a challenge it was for me, a college student, to try and help her! I started by bowing my head and praying for God's guidance, for I didn't know what to say.

"Ruby, you have had a very difficult life," I said softly. "You have turned to many toys of the Devil—such as alcohol, tobacco, romance novels and magazines filled with crime—to hide your sorrow."

"Coming to Jesus means turning away from the world. If you lean on Him, He will give you a new life—a life that is free from these sinful habits."

This was my first experience praying for God's power to transform a person's bad habits into God's lifestyle. I had heard others tell how God, through the working of the Holy Spirit, can give victory over the things of the world. But this time I saw it first hand.

"The things of the world separate us from living with and for God," I told Ruby. "If you want to be baptized and serve Him, all of these things must go."

"How do I start?" Ruby was sincere about wanting to change, but didn't know how to begin.

"First we pray for God's deliverance from these habits," I told her. Then I led her in such a prayer.

"Next we must do our part to keep from being tempted," I explained. "Begin by getting rid of the magazines you have, and don't buy anymore. When you pass by such a magazine rack in the store, go quickly by and make no provision for the flesh."

Ruby also needed to gain the victory over alcohol. She didn't feel that would be a problem, for she wasn't a heavy drinker. But she did have a problem with smoking. Without a doubt, it was her toughest battle.

Ruby and I prayed for the victory every night after the meeting, yet she was having a very hard time with it.

"You need to get rid of the cigarettes you have around the house," I finally told her one evening. "Bring them to me, and I will keep them for you."

"What will I do if I need a smoke?" Ruby wanted to know.

"If you need one so bad you can't stand it any more, come to me," I replied. "Then I will give one to you." And so Ruby agreed, and that truly was it for her. God gave her the victory—Praise His name!

Soon the series was winding down, and we were to the very last week of the meetings. Each night, Pastor Livengood made a call for those who wanted to surrender their lives to Jesus and show it through baptism to come forward.

"I believe I am ready to come forward," Ruby told me before the meeting one night. "Every night when you sing the song, "Pass Me Not O Gentle Savior," the words keep ringing in my mind. I'm not going to let the Savior pass me by while on others He is calling. No, I want to respond to His call."

"If you'll sing that song at the end of the meeting tonight," Ruby told me, "I do think I will come forward." And so that's what we sang, and as we did, Ruby did come forward. It was a very wonderful moment for her, and it was for me, too. I had heard how God could take the life of even a soul who was steeped in many sinful habits, and turn it right around. But this was the first time I had seen such a remarkable transformation for myself. It was the music—combined with solid, Bible-based preaching—that really kept drawing her home. I think God gave me that experience of working with Ruby, together with many other similar experiences, to show me just how important music really is.

### *Notable Quote:*

"Song is one of the most effective means of impressing spiritual truth upon the heart. Often by the words of sacred song, the springs of penitence and faith have been unsealed." (Review & Herald June 6, 1912)

*Pass me not O gentle Savior,*
*Hear my humble cry;*
*While on others Thou art calling,*
*Do not pass me by.*

*Savior, Savior, hear my humble cry,*
*While on others thou art calling,*
*Do not pass me by.*

—Fanny J. Crosby

### Story #4:
### *Baby Francis and the Bullet Holes*

On one particular road trip, when the King's Heralds were traveling in the Dominican Republic, I met a most unforgettable character. It had been a long day, filled with travel and appointments, and we were all very tired. So we were quite happy when our hosts dropped us off at the motel that Friday night.

The lady at the desk gave me the key to a room on the second floor, down at the end of a breezeway. My intention, of course, was to climb into bed as quickly as possible and catch some much-needed shut-eye.

Nothing prepared me for the sight that met my eyes as I flipped on the light in my room, however. The walls were riddled with bullet holes! I wasn't sure what had happened there, but one thing seemed certain: someone was there to get someone!

This made me rather uncomfortable, so I made my way quickly back to the desk and tried to change my room.

"A man named Francis stayed in that room last night," the desk attendant explained. "He was trying to overthrow the government, so the army came to get him."

"Well, they must have got him," I replied. Judging from the number of rounds fired, I felt sure of that!

"Actually, they didn't," the lady told me. "Francis heard they were coming, and escaped just in time."

I asked to change my room, but she said that was the only one she had for me.

"You'll be O.K.," she tried to sound reassuring, adding that they didn't have revolutions *that* often in her country.

I went back to my room and tried to sleep, but all I could see were those holes in the walls.

"What if they come back?" I worried. "I'm such a big target, they surely will hit me!"

I heard every sound the whole night through—plus a few that weren't there. When dawn finally broke, I could hardly wait to get up and get dressed. It was very early, and quite a long time before we were to leave for our next appointment. So I decided to go for a walk.

The hotel was shaped like an "L," so I walked to the corner of the "L" and started down to the first floor. That's when another sight met my eyes—as I looked underneath the room I had stayed in. For there, sitting on three chairs and still hanging over, was the most unusual human being I had ever seen. She had blonde hair, and as I stepped onto the sidewalk she waved.

"Do you speak English?" she asked.

"Yes," I replied, as I looked her over real good.

"Would you like to talk with me?" she asked.

"Sure," I walked over to where she was sitting. She was huge, very huge.

"Would you mind telling me how much you weigh?" I asked.

"847 pounds," she told me.

In the next few minutes I learned that her name was Baby Francis, and she was the fat lady in a circus. She had to buy three airline tickets to travel, and though she was very wide, could still scrape through a door sideways.

Baby Francis had been on every diet imaginable, with the wrong results.

"One time I ate nothing but lettuce and water for three weeks," she told me, "and gained nine pounds."

"You won't be able to help yourself," the doctor had warned, "no matter how hard you try."

Baby Francis had a wonderful personality. She said she came to the Dominican Republic every year with a circus from the States. The people down there loved her, and she loved them too.

I asked her if I could have my picture taken with her so I could show it to my wife. Compared to Baby Francis, she wouldn't think I was very big at all! Baby Francis laughed and said "yes, I would be happy to have my picture taken with you." She also showed me pictures of her husband and daughter, both of whom were normal size.

Her motel room was directly under mine, and I couldn't help but notice the big hole in the wall behind her. So I asked if she knew how it got there.

"Well," she said, "two nights ago there was a man named Francis rooming above me. The army came to get him, but he escaped in time." That's when someone told the army Francis was just below, in her room.

"Since my name is Baby Francis they thought it was me," she sighed. So the army drove up in a tank, and shot a hole in her wall!

"The vibration was so strong," she told me, "it lowered the two double beds I was sleeping on right to the floor. Thank God— the ammunition went right over me, for Jesus protected me."

"Are you a Christian, then?" I wanted to know.

"Oh yes," she replied. "Jesus is my Savior."

I asked if she went to church, but the answer was no. Sadly enough, the last time she'd gone she had broken a pew.

"I don't go to church anymore," she said, "but I have a pastor, and he travels with me while I'm in the States."

"He's showed me the way to Jesus," she went on. "I've taken several Bible courses from him, and plan to take more when I get home."

Then she said something that sent a tingle right up my spine.

"My pastor's name is Richards, out of Los Angeles, California. You should meet him someday! That's my greatest desire—to meet him and tell him what he's meant to me." She went on to say that she'd really like to meet the male choir, also.

Of course, she had no idea who I was or that the quartet was staying in that motel. And I didn't want to tell her—at least, not yet.

"I'll be back soon," I said after we'd talked for a while. "There's someone I want you to meet."

Soon I was back with Jim, Jack and Bob. She still didn't know who we were, but I kind of wanted it that way. You see, there was a very special song the King's Heralds sang at the beginning of each Voice of Prophecy broadcast:

*"Lift up the trumpet, and loud let it ring,*
*Jesus is coming again."*

I knew the minute we sang that song, she'd know. Jack blew the pitch pipe, and as we started in, the most beautiful smile of recognition came across her face while the tears flowed freely down her checks.

When we finished the song, Baby Francis got up from her chairs and came toward us. Her arms were held out wide—wide enough to take us all in—as we huddled together to receive a most wonderful, soft, and loving hug. What a moment of rejoicing that was! Once again, music was the chord that bound us together in the Lord.

We sang several more songs for Baby Francis, and then she requested special prayer.

"When I go back to the States, I'm having surgery," she told us. Baby Francis only had a 50/50 chance of recovery, but without the surgery she had no chance of living very long at all.

We had prayer with Baby Francis, and were able to tell her more about the wonderful Jesus she'd come to love and believe in.

Deep in my heart, I've always known it was a miracle of God's grace that brought us to Baby Francis. And this experience was a real encouragement to me, for after hearing her story, I knew without a doubt that God's grace was big enough to save a soul like hers—all 847 pounds worth.

"Maybe I have a chance, too," I thought to myself, and understood more than ever that we never know what the cause of someone else's problem is.

Elder Richards wasn't with us at the time we met Baby Francis, but we told him her story. He wanted to meet and pray with this dear lady, of course, but it wasn't too long before the Los Angeles Times reported her passing away.

We were saddened to hear of her death, but glad to know she had died in the hope of a resurrection. It encouraged me to think that God cared enough for this one searching soul, no matter how large or small, to bring her and the quartet together, deep down in the Dominican Republic.

### Story #5:
### *Making an Awful Memory*

One memory I would like to forget happened while singing with the King's Heralds on tour in Brazil. I was rooming with Bob Edwards at the time, and we were staying in a very large hotel. Having just finished all the day's singing appointments, we were tired and anxious to get settled for a good night's sleep.

Just before I dozed off, Bob asked if I wanted to go to breakfast with him the next morning.

"I think I'll pass this time," I told him. Having breakfast would mean getting up pretty early, and I was anxious to sleep as long as I could. Bob was already gone by the time I woke up and started getting ready for our usual day of four to six singing programs. I was just ready to leave the room when there was a knock on the door. I opened it to find a bellhop standing there with a tray in his hands that had two hardboiled eggs, and two hard buns.

"Wait 'til Bob hears this," I thought. I was the lucky one after all!

I peeled one of the eggs, stuck it in my mouth whole (just like my mom always told me not to do), and picked up my case. I ran to the elevator to catch up with the rest of the group. We were on the tenth flour of the hotel, and I noticed the elevator was on the eleventh floor, so I was in luck. Here I stood with a whole egg in my mouth, and of course, my mouth was oval-shaped. The door opened and there stood two people in the elevator. They greeted me, and I just nodded to them and hurried to the back corner of the elevator to "work on" the egg. Putting down my brief case, I started to consume it—only to discover that it was rotten to the yolk! Wow, what a flavor! It was horrible, and the smell of it went through my nostrils. Talk about bad breath!

I didn't know what to do with the egg. I didn't want to spit it out in front of the folks on the elevator, so I put it back together as best as I could. The elevator stopped at every floor, until it was jam packed with people. Meanwhile, I was busy devising a plan to get rid of the egg.

Fortunately, there was a back door next to the elevator that led to an alley behind the hotel. My plan was to hurry out there and deposit the egg. But when we came to a stop at the lobby and the doors opened, the driver of the car I was to ride in that day was right there waiting for me!

I tried to ignore him, hoping to slip by and get to the back alley, but he wouldn't allow me to pass. He greeted me, took my arm, and soon we were headed out the front door of the hotel. All the time my mind was wondering what to do with the egg. I decided the next best thing to do would be to step to the curb, and spit it out. As we exited the front door, I took a brisk step toward the curb, but he quickly took my arm and turned me to the left. I saw his wife, a dignified and well-dressed lady, coming down the street. I wasn't going to spit it out in front of her, so like a big, strong American, I swallowed the whole thing. It wasn't long, however, until I realized I had done the wrong thing, for soon I was to see it again!

As the day went on I began to feel a little upset to my stomach. But I made it through the day, and finally we arrived back to the hotel. By now I was thinking I would have to get rid of the egg "once more." I had not mentioned it to the team, hoping it would settle down and pass through the right channels. But that wasn't to be, so I finally told Bob my sad story.

"Go in the bathroom and get rid of it," Bob told me.

" I can't do that!" I replied. You see, all my life, whenever I've lost my dinner, it always affects my vocal chords. Somehow I make such a loud noise that I lose my voice, and then I can't sing for a day or two. At the very best, I would be a bit raspy. Now, this might not matter to a farmer or factory worker, but it means quite a bit when you sing for the King's Heralds Quartet!

I lay there in bed, considering the matter, for quite some time. Bob was already asleep when I finally thought of a strategy which I hoped would settle things down. Unfortunately for Bob, my strategy involved using his bed. He was congenial enough when I woke him up and explained the scheme. Though he couldn't see the humor in this move, he was soon relocated in the easy chair and trying to get back to sleep.

As for myself, I put Bob's bed closer to mine and gave my plan a try. The idea was to put my chest on his bed, my legs on mine, and let my tummy (and the egg) hang somewhere in between. I really did think this might settle the problem, but, much to my chagrin, soon found things getting much worse.

Bob had just drifted back to sleep—though not for long—when I crawled on my hands and knees to the bathroom. I sounded just like a mountain lion, and, of course, it woke him up.

"Are you going to make it?" he wanted to know as he paced back and forth in front of the bathroom door. Later Bob commented that all he could think of at the moment was lights going on in rooms all around us, as sleepy travelers wondered "what in the world is that noise?"

As for me, I was getting rid of the egg, laughing, and crying all at the same time. After a couple more exciting heaves I was feeling much better, and Bob was quite happy to get back in his bed again.

The next day our first appointment was on a television show. Bob and I were in one car, and Jerry and Wayne in another. We arrived at the studio just in time to start the show. Wayne handed us the program, and the first song was "Good News"—which was really "bad news" that morning. That was a song that I started out with a two-note solo. I whispered to Wayne that I couldn't do it, and he assured me I would do okay. We were introduced, the red light came on and Wayne blew the pitch pipe, so I started to sing. It was so raspy that the pitch was even in question. We got through it, but ever after that Wayne always asked me if my voice was okay!

I have tried to come up with a good moral lesson to this story, though it's kind of a stretch. Who knows, maybe that egg was something like rotten music. We shouldn't ingest it in the first place, and if we do, it poisons our entire system. Though it inconveniences our friends or even results in loud noises, there may only be one way to get rid of it. Unpleasant as it seems, it's got to be done. It's so much better, of course, not to swallow those songs in the first place.

## Story #6:
### Candy and the Shoe-Shine Boy

One of the most heartwarming experiences I had while traveling with the King's Heralds happened at a large South American airport. We had stopped to change planes, and had a three-hour layover.

Having ridden in the back seat of the plane (that was closest to the 7-up and other goodies), I was the last one off. As I stood at the top of the stairs, ready to descend, I saw a young boy coming toward the airplane. He was shirtless, shoeless, and sockless. In fact, the only thing he had on was a pair of khaki shorts. He had a box under his arm, and as I walked down the tarmac, I noticed his eyes were on me.

We seemed destined to meet each other, and as I got closer, he gave me a beautiful smile. His teeth were very white, and as near as I could tell, the only thing clean about him. He looked like he hadn't had a bath in weeks, and his hair was messy.

The boy stood in front of me and put his box on the ground. When he took the lid off, I knew what he wanted, for I could see all the shoe polish, rags, and brushes in his box.

Other children were all around me, too, pulling at my coat saying the only word they knew in English: "gimmie." But I was impressed with this boy: he was out working! Since I had plenty of time on my hands, and my shoes could use a good shine, I nodded my approval, and he got out his tools.

I put my foot on his box while he polished, brushed and polished my shoe. Then, looking up with a smile, he tapped under my shoe as if to say "O.K. big fella, give me your other foot."

I watched him as he was working, and decided to test him. So instead of smiling back when he was finished, I scowled and shook my head "no."

I didn't speak his language, nor he mine, so he thought things over. After a moment, he put his fingers back into the wax and put another coat on my shoes. Then he brushed and polished my shoe once more before giving me that sweet smile again. When I scowled once more, he didn't know how to take it. He couldn't leave, for his whole industry was sitting under my foot. So he polished my shoes for the third time, then looked up again, still smiling.

My face had run out of scowls, at least for the moment, so this time I smiled and nodded "yes." He was so relieved, it was written all over his face. No doubt he'd never had such a tough customer in all his young life.

He polished my other shoe three times before looking up for approval, and again I nodded "yes." I needed to pay him now, so I pulled out my change, and nodded for him to choose. There were lots of nickels and dimes to choose from, but no quarters.

He looked them all over, and finally took a nickel. It was the biggest coin I had: he didn't understand that the dimes were worth twice as much. He took it and gave me a big smile, but then he got another scowl from me. I pointed for him to put it back in my hand, and he was very disappointed. It showed all over his face, and I thought I'd soon bring him to tears. He thought I wasn't going to pay him!

Before I left home, I had told my wife I wanted to take some extra money in case I saw a real need. Well, this was a real need. So I put my change back in my pocket, and pulled out two one-hundred dollar bills in his money. I handed it to him and he looked them over. I could see he was thinking. He'd never seen that much money in his life, and probably thought I was just showing him how rich I was. So he handed it back to me as if to say "thanks for letting me see your money, but now may I please have my nickel?"

But I kept giving it back to him, until at last he knew that it was his money to keep. He folded it up into a small package, opened his box, and stuck it under all the junk he had inside.

We went inside the airport together, and I had a boy for three hours. He took his box over to the corner where he kept it when he wasn't working. After returning to me he stuck closer than a brother. We couldn't speak the same language, so I couldn't ask his name or anything about his life. All we could do was smile at each other. Once he reached up and took my hand, and I couldn't help but think about all that shoe polish. My hand would look like a zebra. But soon I forgot about the shoe polish, as he squeezed it and looked up as if to say, "I'll be your boy, please take me home with you."

That would have been fun, of course. I would have folded him right into my suitcase, and when I got home to greet Patsy, out would jump this dirty, smelly, little boy. I know what she would have done. She would have put him in the bathtub, got out a potato brush and scrubbed him up real good, and put clean clothes on him. Then she would send him to school, God's school, the only place for our kids. But I knew this would not be possible. He had a mother and dad who loved him. They would watch over him as best they could, so I knew I couldn't adopt him.

So I bought him a candy bar instead. It was a big one, a Nestles, the kind you used to pay 29 cents for.

"Maybe it's been a long time since he had one," I thought as he sniffed it. That's when I realized, he'd never eaten a candy bar before. I motioned for him to try it, but he wouldn't open it up. Maybe he was afraid he wouldn't like it, or felt embarrassed. So he just held on to it tightly, as if to say "thanks."

We visited a basket shop next. There were straw baskets there of all shapes and sizes, beautifully woven together. The lady was trying to sell me her wares when I noticed my boy had turned back. I knew what he was doing, for I'm very familiar with the sound of a candy bar wrapper being ripped very slowly.

Soon he had a corner of the candy uncovered. Then he broke off a piece and put it in his mouth. You have to know what happened next—the sweet chocolate began to melt, the taste buds took over, and "Wow! What a treat!"

This is what happened to my friend, and soon he turned back around. It was so good that the tears started spilling out the corner of his eyes, and onto the floor. When I saw how happy he was, I got teary-eyed too. So I drew him close to me and put my arms around him.

I couldn't help myself, I just had to pray for him.

"Dear Lord," I prayed, "please send someone to this boy who can speak his language. Have them tell him about You, and the plan of salvation You gave us. Tell him about the cross, tell him about the resurrection, and Your soon coming to take us home."

Somehow, I have faith that this will happen, and I hope to him in the kingdom. As soon as I said "Amen," he took off running across the airport. Maybe I embarrassed him, I thought. But I watched every move he made, and saw that he went to his box and put the candy bar in it.

Then he took something from the box, and ran back to me, his fist doubled up. There was something in his hand, but I had no idea what it might be. He had so much junk in that box it could have been a lot of things, maybe even a toad. He motioned for me to put out my hand, and he slowly opened his fist and put something in my hand. It wasn't a toad, it was a little piece of hard native candy. It was unwrapped, and even looked like he'd sucked on it for a while. It had little feathers all over it, and he urged me to eat it, using the same sign language I'd used on him.

"What will I do with this candy?" I thought. I didn't dare put it in my mouth, for fear it might be the end of my trip, or the beginning of many! So, I wrapped it in a piece of paper, stuck it in my pocket, and patted it as if to say "I want to keep this."

Our three hours together passed all too quickly. The announcement for boarding my plane soon blared over the speakers, and my little friend walked with me right up to the door. He stood there, with his little hands on the glass, and waved good-bye to me with tears in his eyes. I'll never forget that picture, of my little friend saying good-bye. Yes, it is etched in my mind forever.

"Lord, why did you let me fall in love with that little boy," I wanted to know as I buckled up my seatbelt on the plane. "I don't even know his name, yet what a wonderful time we had." And once again I asked God for the privilege of seeing that cheerful young lad in the kingdom.

Later that night I told the missionary family I stayed with about my experience at the airport that day. I also showed them the piece of candy.

The response of my host was very startling to me.

"Children in this country are so poor," he told me. "They often leave home with only a piece of candy to suck on throughout the day. When they get home at night, they get one bowl of rice and beans."

The missionary's next thought was a life-changing one for me.

"You gave a lot to that little boy," he told me. "More than he would make in a year's time. Even the candy bar was something he could never afford. He wanted to give something back to you, so he gave you everything he had—one piece of candy."

That's when my mind went back to a favorite Bible verse.

"We love Him because He first loved us." (1 John 4:19)   This whole experience gave me a new understanding of what this text really means.  I could never give anyone enough to compare, or even begin to compare, with what God has given me.  Yet He allowed me to sense the joy of reaching out and giving love to this boy. That is the way God works, for when we try to reach out and love someone without any thought of return, when we try to make someone happy just for the joy of it, that's when God can better help us understand His great, magnificent, unselfish love for us.

### Story #7:
### On the Road With H.M.S. Richards, Sr.

During my years with the King's Heralds quartet, we traveled almost exclusively by car. This made it easier for us to stop at various points across the country, and Elder Richards took advantage of this fact to visit many of his radio audience.

He kept a card file of people who had asked him to come and see them. Then, if we traveled within a reasonable distance of their home, we would call on them.

One night, as we checked into our motel, the Chief announced he wanted to visit a lady who had been listening to the broadcast for over twenty years. She had requested a visit from the team, but she lived about one hundred miles off the route we were taking. This upset me a little; I did not look forward to rising early the next day, and driving two hundred extra miles for just one person.

We arrived at the address to find a little, old lady. She had been bed-ridden for many years. There she lay, all shriveled up with arthritis. Something about this experience really made an impression on me; I shall never forget the few minutes we spent with her.

"You told me you'd come, and you're here," she told Elder Richards. We sang a few songs for her, and some that she requested. The Chief read some comforting Scriptures to her. Then he knelt by her bed and poured out his heart in prayer for her. What a wonderful experience it was! We left with tears in our eyes, tears of joy for the privilege of meeting this dear lady, and I was so grateful we did take the time to go and visit her.

Elder H.M.S. Richards, Sr. was a man of faith, and he lived by it. One time during my first year with the quartet, the Voice had a real crisis over finances. Elder Richards told us that we were $100,000 short at the end of that year, and we met for worship Monday morning to talk about the need.

"I want to praise God for His faithfulness to our radio ministry," Elder Richards said, "and all the many blessings we've had this year." Then he told us he was going to pray for the financial needs of the ministry.

"If there are any doubters present," he urged, "I ask you to leave before I pray." I was a bit uneasy about this. I wasn't sure what to think, but didn't think it would look good for the newest member of the quartet to get up and walk out. One thing I did know—God had already answered many prayers for us that year. I could not move out of my seat, for my experience at the Voice so far gave me faith to believe it could happen again.

Then Elder Richards poured out his heart to the Father, and what a prayer it was. Everyone in the room was very still, for we were all involved in the prayer. I felt the presence of the Holy Spirit in the room that day, and sensed the assurance of the still, small voice.

The next week we left on a trip to Oregon, and on up the west coast. After our first meeting in Portland, we returned to our motel. There the Chief received a phone call from his secretary, telling him of a letter he had gotten that day from one of our listeners in Boston. She sent a Christmas gift of $5,000 each year to the Voice, but this year she sent $30,000.

"I feel like the radio broadcast is in special need," she wrote, "so I'm sending an extra $25,000." And so it went through the entire trip. He just kept getting phone calls, until the entire $100,000 was in the treasury.

It always amazed me how God would send us what we needed, then the money stopped 'til the next need arose.

The Chief never begged for money; he depended, by faith, on Box 55 for continuing financial support. We were a part of the General Conference and had several ordained ministers on staff, but Elder Richards never received tithe money to pay for their salaries.

Another rewarding experience happened once when we were in Philadelphia, Pennsylvania. We were just checking into a motel that night when the Chief once again announced he wanted to rise a little early the next morning. There was an elderly couple he wanted to visit. They had been listening to the broadcast for twenty-five years, and he had promised to visit and pray with them if he ever got close.

We found them living on the tenth floor of a high-rise retirement center. The Chief rang the doorbell, and we heard feet shuffling across the floor. The door opened, and the lady quickly recognized Elder Richards from his picture in the Voice of Prophecy News. She was very excited to see him, and ushered us in.

The lady's husband was back in the bedroom, but she soon brought him out in a wheelchair. Then, after we had gotten acquainted, Elder Richards fell to his knees and prayed for this couple. He also spoke words of spiritual encouragement, and the quartet sang.

"We must be going," the Chief said after a while, for we had several appointments to keep that day.

"Just a minute," the lady told him. "We have something for you." Then she went back into the bedroom and pulled a paper bag from under the bed.

"You are our church," she told us. "You are our preacher, and you are our choir. So every week during church we put a little offering in the sack for you. We thought if you ever came to see us, we'd give it to you."

The Chief thanked them for their offering, and we left. Later, when we counted the money, we found more than $3,000 in the bag. Of course, we hadn't stopped to visit this couple because we knew about the money. We had stopped because of the interest the Chief had in encouraging and praying with them. But God blessed his act of faith with yet another gift of support for the ministry of the Voice of Prophecy.

Another story that comes to mind happened right at our home base of Glendale, California. Elder Richards liked to walk the mile or so to the office, and he would use this time for reading.

He knew all the dogs in the area, and would always speak to them. He also carried a water pistol with him filled with ammonia, just in case he ran across some dog in need of a little training.

The Chief was walking home after a recording session one day when a car pulled up beside him. It was Elder Richards doctor.

"Would you like a ride?" the doctor rolled down his window and smiled at the Chief.

"My doctor says I should walk," Elder Richards replied.

"Well, I want to ask you a question," the doctor said. So the Chief climbed into the car.

"What's new at the Voice?" the doctor wanted to know.

"Well, I've been praying for an opportunity to broadcast out of Tijuana, Mexico," came back the reply. "There's a huge radio station there that the whole nation can hear at night. Just think of it! All the truckers could hear the message while they're out driving at night."

"Herbert W. Armstrong has written the station, and they'll let him on for $50,000 a year. But they'd rather have us, so they've offered to let us have the airtime for $25,000 per year."

The doctor pulled his car over to curb, and the tears began to flow freely as he gave his testimony.

"My mother just passed away, and left $25,000," he told the Chief. "I don't need it, so I prayed this morning for God's guidance in what to do with the money. I wanted to know what special project it should be used for, and now I know—you'll be on Tijuana radio!"

Pastor Richards' whole radio ministry was full of stories like this, and God rewarded his faith by supplying the needed funds.

One time, on my first campmeeting tour, I discovered I was running low on cash. I knew people were always stuffing Pastor Richards pockets with money, so I asked him if he would cash a twenty-five dollar check. I will never forget his reaction to my request.

"That's God's money," he told me. "I won't touch it, for the treasury has to count it and put it in the budget for operation."

But he did offer to cash my check with a little extra of his own money. He didn't have much, for he put everything he could into the broadcast. He even refinanced his humble home when it was near payoff, to put more money back into the Voice. What a dedication he had to his calling, his example in this and many other areas has always been an inspiration to me.

### Story #8 :
### *Man of Great Prayer and Faith (Part I)*

Elder Richards always showed such love and tenderness to other people. He received calls from all over the world for prayer, and he would pray for these people every Thursday morning at the Voice prayer request service.

We would take turns leading out in this service, and it was our privilege to go through the request box and read the letters. That was quite an experience; each week we would read a few samples of the request in worship, then pray for those people as a group. And they were not just quick prayers. No, many of the Voice family would earnestly pray for every request.

Many times, when we were on the road, people would ask for prayer and anointing. I had the privilege of being with the Chief for several times when this service was conducted, and it was a real thrill to hear him encourage the people about God's healing.

"You will be healed," he assured them, explaining that some would be instantly, some over a period of time, and some at the resurrection.

"You can know your prayers will be answered," he would say. "But we must leave the timing up to God." He never talked about prayer and anointing results, for he knew it was God's power, not his, that performed any miracle. But his faith was great in God's power, and there was healing according to God's will and timing.

One doctor in particular stands out in my mind. He couldn't practice medicine any more due to the crippling arthritis in his hands, so he asked for prayer. I met that doctor many years later, and he showed me how God had healed him. He was still practicing medicine.

I experienced healing myself while at the Voice. The team was in Hawaii, the pastor wanted to take us to see some black sand on our day off. I wasn't interested in black sand, I wanted to go to the beach instead. There was a big beach just across from our motel, so I stayed behind and had a peaceful day all to myself.

There was no one on the beach but me, and I had a wonderful time splashing around in the ocean.

The next day we flew back to California for an upcoming camp-meeting. It was then that I began to feel a little sore in my left foot, and asked a doctor about it.

"You have an infection there," he told me, then instructed me to rub the top of the sore with soap and water then cover it with a Band-Aid. That was very hard to do, but I finally got it done. The foot seemed better the next day, and in two days we flew home. The foot started to bother me again, however, so I called my doctor in Glendale.

"That doesn't look too good," the doctor remarked, and told me to soak the foot several times in Epson salts. The next morning he checked it again, and put me in the hospital.

The doctors ran some tests, and decided I had gotten a staff infection from rubbing my foot against a coral reef.

I had not called the Chief at this point, for I didn't want to upset him. I did tell the other members of the quartet that I would probably be in the hospital for a couple of weeks.

We were scheduled to leave on Wednesday to drive to the Missouri campmeeting. I was laying in my hospital bed at about 6 a.m. on the day of our scheduled departure when I heard these big footsteps coming down the hall. I had a feeling it was the Chief, and I was right.

"What are you doing here?" he wanted to know as he entered my room. "Don't you know we have to go on a journey today?"

"Yes, Chief," I told him. "But as you can see my foot is all bandaged up. The doctor says it could be two more weeks before I can rejoin the team."

"How long have you had this infection?" he wanted to know.

"Three days," I replied.

"Three days and you never told me?" The Chief was incredulous. "Three days I could have been praying for you." With that he fell to his knees and started to pray.

"Dear Lord we're leaving this morning to do your work, and John is not with us. Please heal him so that he can join us Friday night in Missouri."

"See you Friday," he said, getting up.

But Chief, you don't understand," I argued. "The doctor says it will be at least two weeks."

"Where is your faith?" he wanted to know. "Don't you believe the Lord wants us together this weekend?"

"Yes, Chief," I responded. "And I'll pray, too."

That night he called me from his motel room.

"Bow your head," he told me. "We are going to pray."

"Lord, it isn't for our glory, but for Yours, that I pray for John," he pleaded. "Please bring us together for the meeting Friday night, and thank You for hearing our prayer, Amen."

"See you Friday night," he reminded me, and I didn't have the heart to repeat what the doctor had said that day. My foot was not getting better!

Thursday night the phone rang, and once again it was the Chief. Once more he poured out his heart in behalf of the work, asking God to bring the team together for Friday night.

"See you tomorrow night," he told me as soon as he said amen, he reminded me to "Have faith in God."

The doctor had a long day Thursday, so he didn't reach my room until just before midnight.

"How are you doing?" he wanted to know.

"Just fine, Doc," I replied. Taking the bandage off my foot, he looked at it, felt all around it, and asked if it hurt anymore.

"No, it doesn't hurt," I told him.

"Well, your infection is gone," he said. "As far as I'm concerned, you can fly and rejoin with the team."

What a thrilling moment that was in my life! I knew I had experienced healing through the Chief's faith and the wonderful power of God.

Mr. Gillis, our office manager, quickly found me a flight to St. Louis, and arranged for me a ride from the airport to the campground. As it turned out, I arrived just a short time before the meeting.

The Chief was in the minister's room with his back to me when I walked in. I slipped my hand in his arm to let him know I was there. When the Chief saw me, he pulled out his pocket watch and looked at it.

"You cut that kind of close," he said. He wasn't surprised or shocked, just thankful to God for answering his prayers.

I know if God had chosen not to heal me, it wouldn't have shaken the Chief's faith. Yet he knew, that if my being healed was in God's will, it would be done.

Somehow I believe that the eleventh chapter of Hebrews, that Hall of Faith where the great believers of the Bible are listed, is not closed yet. I believe that someday, another name will be added to that list. "By faith H.M.S. Richards, Sr...."

Yes, he lived his life by prayer and faith

### Story #9:
### *Man of Great Prayer and Faith (Part II)*

Though I've already mentioned a number of my experiences working for and with the Chief, as we called H.M.S. Richards, Sr., there are a few more things I really must say. I'm not exactly sure how to describe this man of God, but I'm going to try.

The first dimension of his life I would speak to was his relationship with God. Elder Richards made it his custom to reach for his Bible as soon as he awoke each day. In fact, he wouldn't get up until he had read the Word.

The first time I stayed overnight at Elder Richards home, I had an early flight out the next morning. I tried to say good-bye the night before, but the Chief wouldn't hear of my leaving until we had prayer together.

The next morning I tried to be as quiet as a mouse as I got myself around. When I was finally ready to leave, I nearly tripped over him as I started down the hall. He was lying across the hallway, reading his Bible.

When he saw me, he got up and we went into the next room. There he prayed a parting prayer for me. As always, it was a wonderful experience to pray with this godly man.

Elder Richards read the entire Bible through every year. Sometimes he read it more than once, and for many years he read the New Testament through every month.

He always rode in the front seat as we traveled, reading almost continually. On one of our road trips, I remember asking him about one verse in the New Testament that troubled me at the time.

"Would you please explain this to me?" I asked, and read him the verse.

"You must go back to the beginning of the chapter if you want to understand," he told me. "Then read to the end of it." I had not told him where the verse was found, but he quoted the reference from memory.

Many times while preaching the Chief would look at his Bible as if he were reading from it, but he would be quoting rather than reading because of his poor eyesight. Elder Richards memorized great portions of Scripture, and he truly loved God's Word.

H.M.S., Sr., was an avid reader of other books as well. Some of you may be old enough to remember the large metal rack that was on top of the King's Heralds station wagon. There were three compartments in it. The second one held our suits and shoes. The third one held other important things. But the first compartment held books the Chief wanted to read as we traveled.

"Reading is my indoor sport," he used to say.

Elder Richards eyes had been injured in an accident when he was still a young boy, and he only had one eye to read with. This injury kept him from playing sports with his classmates, for he couldn't see well enough to catch a ball. And so reading became his life.

You couldn't find a subject he wasn't at least somewhat acquainted with. His knowledge extended from jet engines, to wars, to biographies of great world leaders, as well as great preachers and religious leaders. He read about God's music, and the stories of favorite hymns, travel, history, medicine, proper diet—and the list goes on.

Before my time, the King's Heralds had built H.M.S. a study behind his house where he could keep his books. He had a huge library and he really did read all the books, some of them more than once. He also subscribed to many magazines, including some on science, medicine, and the latest inventions.

Elder Richards was a firm believer in the Spirit of Prophecy, and read the Conflict of the Ages series through many times. Of course, he read Ellen White's other writings as well.

"These are the best books to help you understand Scripture," he often told me, especially as I was preparing to leave the quartet and go into the ministry. "If you read and re-read this series, you will gain new understandings of this wonderful message."

When the SDA Bible Commentary first came out, Elder Richards sat down and read it from cover to cover. He also read most of the books that came off the press from the two church publishing houses. He was asked by many Adventist writers to read and check their book before printing it.

Elder Richards was an avid reader of the church periodicals as well. He also studied the lives of many great preachers along with the books they had written. He especially loved to read about John Wesley. He had volumes about this man, and would often tell us interesting facts about his life story.

When we were in Michigan, the Chief always wanted to visit his favorite religious bookstore. The name of the store was Kregel's, and it was in Grand Rapids. Elder Richards and Mr. Kregel became great friends. When the Chief wanted to find a book out of print, Mr. Kregel would find it for him. He also made a bed for Elder Richards, downstairs in the store. That way, the Chief could stay all night and choose new books to read. The rest of the team would go to the motel to sleep, then pick the Chief up the next morning. Sometimes he'd have a large stack of books to buy, but couldn't afford them all. Then he had a hard time choosing which ones to take and which to leave for another time.

I must mention his gift of writing, both books, and poems. Here are just a few titles of some of his many books.

1. Revival Sermons by H.M.S. Richards, Sr. (1947) This was the first of many books of his sermons through the years.
2. The Stars and the Bible (1952)

Poem he wrote in this book:

*I Saw His Hand*

I saw the glory of His robe
    Star-spangled in the dome of night,
Where fold on fold the Milky Way
    Spreads out its glowing arch of light
I saw His finger light-the flame
    Of red Andromeda's million suns,
And touch Polaris into fire
    While the glittering wheel of Virgo runs.
I saw His name, Creator, writ
    In far star-cities swinging high;
Beyound Aldebaran's ruddy glow
    I saw His Hand across the sky.
I saw Him bind the Pleiades

And guide Arcturus with his train,
Where cold Orion's starry sword
   Makes all our little grandeur vain.
I saw His anger lash and burn
   Around the sun's corona glow;
By Him the planets wheel and turn—-
   Are never fast and never slow.
I saw Him in the depths of space,
   Behind the dark night's farthest rim,
Where shout the sons of God with joy
   Some new creation's glory hymn.
I saw His rainbow throne of light
   Reflect in star-clouds vast and dim;
I saw the thunder of His power,
   But never knew the love of Him.
I never knew until I saw
   A thorn-crowned Man bear all my loss;
I gave my heart to Him because
   I saw His Hand upon the cross.

                         H. M. S. Richards, Sr.

3. *Christmas Catechism* (1953)

I Thank Thee Lord . . .
I thank Thee, Lord, that Jesus came
   In far Judea long ago;
That He was born and lived and died
   To heal our woe.
I thank Thee He will come again
   In clouds all glorious to behold;
The He will gather then His sheep
   Into His fold.
But more—far more—I thank Thee, Lord,
   That Jesus comes when all is dim
And holds this trembling heart of mine
   In love with Him.

*4.* What Jesus Said (1957)
*5.* Look To The Stars (1964)
*6.* Why I Am A Seventh-Day Adventist (1965)
*7.* One World (1972)

These are just a few examples of the many books written by Elder Richards. It must be noted that every book he wrote centered around this wonderful message for the last days.

Elder Richards had a very nice bass voice, and he sang with enthusiasm during our song services and our meetings. It was a grand experience to stand beside him, hearing the depths of feeling he put into songs.

One of the thrills of my years at the Voice was to record a song with him for the broadcast. The song was F.E. Belden's, "Look For The Waymarks." He joined us on the last chorus, and it is still a joy to listen to that recording after all these years.

Elder Richards helped me understand more fully the value and power of hymns and gospel songs. He often spoke of how many decisions were made for Jesus after the Word was spoken and the appeal made.

Often, it was a simple song used by the Holy Spirit that brought many souls to a decision to follow Christ. It always amazed me how he would get up after we had sung a song and tell the story of the writer. Sometimes he would give a short life sketch, or the background of the hymn. His view of the author was not shallow. He would read all he could find about him or her.

One song I particularly remember him talking about was "Glorious Things of Thee Are Spoken," by John Newton. What a story that was! Elder Richards had read several books on John Newton's life, and I became so interested in the topic that I bought his biography as well. This was the beginning of my interest in the biography's of writers and composers.

One of Elder Richards favorite songs was Harriet Beecher Stowe's, "'Still, Still, With Thee." I can't tell it like the Chief could, but I'll try to give you some of his thoughts.

Harriet Beecher Stowe was the wife of a famous preacher. She had a daily routine of rising early in the morning to study God's Word and pray for her children, her husband and his ministry. Early one morning, after studying her Bible, she penned the words to this poem which is especially unique because it speaks of the second coming of Christ in soft, tender tones.

> *Still, still with Thee, when purple morning breaketh,*
> *When the bird waketh, and the shadows flee;*
> *Fairer than morning, lovelier than the daylight,*
> *Dawns the sweet consciousness, I am with Thee!*
>
> *Alone with Thee, amid the mystic shadows.*
> *The solemn hush of nature newly born;*
> *Alone with Thee, in holy adoration,*
> *In the calm dew and freshness of the morn.*
>
> *When sinks the soul, subdued by toil, to slumber,*
> *Its closing eye looks up to Thee in prayer;*
> *Sweet the repose beneath Thy wings o'ershading,*
> *But sweeter still, to wake and find Thee there.*
>
> So shall it be at last, in that bright morning,
> When the soul waketh, and life's shadows flee;
> Oh, in that hour, fairer than daylight dawning,
> Shall rise the glorious thought, I am with Thee.

How could anyone add to these beautiful words of relationship with one's God? Elder Richards loved this song, and music in general. Early in his ministry he knew a quartet would be a blessing to the special work God had called him to.

After the Chief had retired and had a stroke, the old quartet visited him in the hospital, and sang this song to him. Wayne asked him to tell us the story again and he never missed a beat. In fact, he sang it with us. This was a special moment for us, and our eyes became misty, thinking of that great day of heaven when we will be able to spend all eternity with God, His holy angels, and the saved throughout eternity—including the Chief.

### Story #10:
### Personal Times with the Chief

One of the most special moments with Elder Richards was when he called me one day to express his desire to see me ordained to the Gospel ministry. He wanted to know if I would object to his recommending me for ordination to the Southern California Conference to take place at the upcoming campmeeting in Long Beach, California. I was speechless to think this man of faith would be the one to recommend me. It is such a high honor to be ordained.

Not only did he recommend me, but at the service he laid his hands on me as we were set apart for ministry. Patsy looked so sweet that day as we accepted the challenge of being faithful to our calling. She has been the best helpmate in the ministry. In fact, her counsel to me through the years has kept me in the path of duty.

Visiting with the Chief in his study from time to time was such a blessing to me. He taught me so much about books and gave me encouragement to follow God's leading, and how to know His will. I remember one time I took some friends with me to his study, and their daughter and son in-law were there, too. They had their little boy with them and they asked the Chief if he would pray for him. He prayed such a dedicatory prayer that all of us were in tears. He held him in his arms and talked to him after the prayer.

"Son, I am an old man now," he told the boy. "When you grow up I will be resting, waiting for Jesus to come. But when we all get home with God I want to look you up so you can tell me how God led you in serving Him."

Our son Gary was in a bad auto accident his senior year of academy, and was not expected to live. We called the Chief that night, and he fell on his knees and prayed for him. When Gary left the hospital six months later he was on crutches and paralyzed from his right knee down. The next school year Elder Richards came to his academy to have a spiritual weekend with the youth.

"God may be calling some of you to be ministers," Elder Richards said to the boys in his last talk. "If He calls, will you be willing to give your life for ministry?"

I shall never forget the moment I saw Gary rise from his chair to answer that call, crutches and all. Today, he is the president of the Northern New England Conference of Seventh-day Adventists.

After leaving the King's Heralds quartet, I led three trips to the Holy Land for Elder Richards. Usually, two bus loads of people signed up to go. It would take a long time to tell all the stories, but let me share this one thing with you. Every day we toured, and at night the chief would explain what we had seen and give us a preview of the next day's journey. The tour guides would come to the meetings just to learn from him. What a blessing he was to the tour group. Elder Richards would take us to places the guides had never seen or heard about.

Some years later, when Elder Richards had grown quite old, the telephone rang in my Texas home. It was the Chief, calling from California.

"John, I am not feeling well today," he told me. "I'm calling to ask you to pray for me." To tell you the truth, I felt amazed that a man known around the world, a man who could have called many more important people to pray for him, for whatever reason chose to call me that night. And so I offered a simple prayer asking for healing, and shared some encouraging words. Elder Richards was in his eighties then, but he still made the effort to send me a warm letter of love and appreciation. I thank the Lord for the privilege of knowing him. Elder Richards had no ego about his extensive knowledge or the great work he had done, but in his shy way he let me know that he loved me.

## Story #11:
## *Singing for Beauty Contestants*

One summer, while working for the Carolina Conference, one of my youth groups had the opportunity to sing for the Miss South Carolina Beauty Pageant. The contestants were having breakfast together, and, as you can imagine, were all made up for the day's activities.

Our team gave them a program of music and testimony that lasted about forty-five minutes, and as the Lord spoke to their hearts, some of them started to weep.

"You can all be winners in Christ," one of our team members told them as we neared the end of our program. Our last song was an invitation to know Jesus:

"Do you know my Jesus, do you know my Friend?" we asked them in song. "Have you heard He loves you, and that He will abide to the end?" Their tears kept flowing and their mascara flowed right along with it, until they were quite a sight!

We were able to visit with them after the closing prayer, and the remark of one contestant has always stayed with me.

"I'm a Christian," she told our team, "and, to tell you the truth, I'd rather be witnessing with you than competing in this pageant."

The lady who invited the team to sing was Gloria Bond, C.E.O. of a large department store. Gloria had been raised an Adventist, but later left the church. The message of God through these young people touched her so deeply, however, that she has since been rebaptized and is now an officer in her church.

We happened to see one of the beauty contestants a few days later, when we were singing in a nearby mall.

"Thanks again for coming to our breakfast," she told us. "We girls had a meeting that night after you left, and decided to become a team that would cheer each other on rather than focusing so much on self."

"You showed us how we could all be winners in Christ Jesus," she told us. Her testimony made us all very happy and thankful for what the Lord had done through our music.

## Story #12:
### *The Day the Church Started Out Empty*

One day I received a phone call from a Methodist minister pastoring in a large southern city.

"Would you be interested in bringing your team to take the first service on Sunday?" he asked me. He said nothing about the second service, so I assumed he was trying us out before making such a commitment.

"My people will be dressed for whatever activities they have planned for the day," he told me during the course of our conversation. The golfers would be coming in their golf attire, and the fishermen would be dressed to go fishing, and they would all be ready for an afternoon of relaxation after church.

We were thankful for the opportunity to witness, so I told him we would come.

"Are you going to play loud music?" the pastor wanted to know when we arrived at the church and started setting up our equipment.

"No," we replied, and explained that we were a small group. "The sound system is used to balance and blend our voices," we assured him, "not to blare our music."

"Be sure to start right on time at 8:30," he instructed. He planned for us to sing a few songs, then he would preach. If there was time at the end he might call on us to sing again.

8:30 came, and there wasn't a single person in the church save our group and the pastor.

"Now you can start to sing," he told us as he walked down the aisle toward the back of the church. "The Lord is here!" Then he left us all alone, without one soul to sing to.

That was a different feeling, to be sure, but we introduced ourselves to the empty church and started to sing. About halfway through our first song one family walked in and sat down to our left.

After the song the father said "Amen," and that gave us a bit of courage. At least we had one family to sing to! Some time during the second song another family walked in, and they too gave a good solid "Amen!" Even more came in during our third song, and by the time our part of the program was over, nearly two hundred people sat in the sanctuary.

In just a few minutes the associate pastor, and soon after that the head pastor came in. We sang two or three more songs, and then turned the program over to the pastor.

"I have made a decision," he announced to the congregation. "I have decided not to preach today."

"Well, amen to that!" said the associate pastor. Then the head pastor turned the remainder of the program over to us!

Only a few of our team members were present at the time, for some had gone home for a break. So we really didn't have that much music to sing to them. But we started to pray individually, and I asked some of the team to do solos. Then we taught the congregation some of the beautiful choruses we have known in the Adventist faith throughout the years, and their hearts were turned to the Lord. When we saw their eyes light up the way they did, we knew they hadn't experienced anything like this before.

"Pastor, surely we have gone on long enough," I finally said. "We are nearing the time for Sunday School."

The pastor turned to the audience. "I think we should go right through Sunday School," he told them. "What do you think?"

"Amen!" It seemed everyone in the congregation was in agreement. The pastor looked at his watch then back at me.

"O.K.," he said. "You have another hour and a half!"

You know, I truly believe that the Lord leads in these situations. When He gives you the chance to witness you have to rely on Him fully. We weren't prepared for another hour and a half, but we sang some more for them. Then I gave a sermonette. Finally I turned to the pastor once more.

"I think we have gone long enough," I told him. "These people have been so kind and patient with us." Then the team lead the congregation in singing "Side by Side We Stand," and the pastor closed with an appeal.

"My heart has really been touched this morning," he told the congregation. "I wonder how many of you would like to follow me to the altar, committing your life anew to Jesus Christ?"

He walked to the altar, waving his arm for those who wished to follow. That's when every person in the church came forward, many with tears in their eyes. The pastor then invited the people to kneel for prayer and express their love to the Lord.

I will never forget the first prayer, that of an elderly lady.

"Dear Savior," she started in, "we have prayed so long that your Spirit might come and move our hearts to repentance, commitment, and love. And now, Lord, you've sent these young people to do that for us today. We don't even know who they are Lord, where they come from, or what their names are. But You sent them as an answer to our request for a repentant spirit in this church."

It was such a thrill to hear that prayer, and to realize that because we'd introduced ourselves when the church was still empty, these people didn't even know who we were.

"Lord, You know how drunk I was last night," prayed a gentleman, kneeling near the altar. "I was in pitiful condition, even saying I never wanted to attend church again. I was fed up with church, Lord, but you woke me up this morning anyway. You wouldn't let me sleep, and told me I'd better get to church. So I finally got up and now I know why. Lord, you've sent these people to show us your true Spirit, and I want to come back to You."

Prayer after prayer gave praise and glory to God for His Spirit and Power. When the service was over the congregation still didn't know who we were! But they did seem certain of one thing, we had been sent there by God!

After I had returned home I received a call from a man in the congregation.

"Mr. Thurber," he said, "I was wondering where you lived and what you do? So I called my preacher and asked for your phone number."

"I'm a Seventh-day Adventist preacher," I replied, and the young people were also Seventh-day Adventists."

There was a long pause on the other end of the line after that.

"I am going to ask our pastor to announce who you are," the man finally said. "I want the whole congregation to know that Seventh-day Adventist youth came and led us into a commitment—a commitment that we have needed for a long, long time."

A few weeks later the pastor called and asked if we would come and sing for his congregation again. He had so many requests; he wanted us to take both the 8:30 and 11:00 services.

It was our privilege to go back, and have another similar experience. We gave God all the glory for this, for there was no power in us save His Spirit working in and through us.

### Story #13:
### *Music and My Mom*

As I mentioned in the introduction of this book, my parents enjoyed good music and taught me to love it at an early age. Music was a special bond that made us closer than ever, and this was true even at the end of my mother's life. Mom was in the wheelchair at the nursing home dining room, and we were alone. She had Alzheimers and couldn't talk, though she seemed to know who I was.

I asked her questions on that day, but she didn't respond. So I held her and kissed her many times, telling her that I loved her. There was still no response, though I really wanted to see one. Then I got an idea.

"Mom," I told her, "I want to sing some of the songs you taught me as a child." I started with:

> *"Rock-a-bye baby in the tree top,*
> *When the wind blows the cradle will rock,*
> *When the bough breaks the cradle will fall,*
> *And down will fall cradle, baby and all."*

She looked at me then, but still had no response. But when I started to sing "Jesus Loves Me," she started to sing too, and never missed a note. This thrilled my heart, of course, for it seemed as if God had opened a window of our past. What joy flooded my soul as she leaned over and kissed me. We both shed a tear, before going on to sing together "My Jesus I Love Thee" and "Abide With Me"—two of her favorite songs. After singing several more songs, I had her repeat some favorite texts with me. She never missed a beat as we went through John 3:16, John 14:1-3, 1 John 1:9, Psalms 23 and many more. It was a thrilling time, that last visit I had with my mother, for very soon after our visit she was laid to rest.

I'm retired now, but I don't believe I'll stop singing as long as God gives me breath. I'm looking forward to heaven, too, for I have several appointments there. One is with my Dad, but I also plan to meet Mom, brother Wayne, H.M.S. Richards, Sr. and H.M.S. Richards, Jr., and millions of other faithful some day on the Sea of Glass.

There we'll raise our voices in one mighty chorus, just as Elder Ted Carcich described so vividly in a sermon I heard nearly 50 years ago. And by God's grace—not because of anything I've ever said or done—I plan to spend the endless ages of eternity singing in God's heavenly choir.

## Story #14:
### *Thoughts on the Sea of Glass*

Have you thought that soon, very soon, will be the most glorious moment in this world's history when Jesus returns to take His children home? Have you thought about the joy, of the host of heaven singing to the redeemed, as we are ushered into heaven? What about singing with the angels, and all the redeemed, with Christ as our choir director? What about the angels folding their wings as the redeemed sing the victorious, Song of Redemption? What about the song of, Moses and the Lamb? What about seeing our Savior, face to face? What about eternal peace, the end of evil, temptation and sin?

"God grant, dear reader, that when Jesus shall come the second time, you may be found ready and waiting; that you may be of that number who shall sing the Song of Redemption around the great white throne, casting their crowns at the feet of the Redeemer. God grant that, with all the redeemed, you may have the glorious privilege of standing upon the Sea of Glass and walking the streets of gold. God grant, that at that time, there may be given to your hand a harp of gold, and that as you sweep its strings all Heaven may resound with your notes of joy and praise." (Signs of the Times, November 10, 1887)

I want to be there, and I long for my family to be there, and all of you my brothers, and sisters. What a day that will be! The provision has been made, it is up to us to repent, and forsake our sins. See you on the Sea of Glass!